Clarice Lispector

Twayne's World Authors Series

Latin American Literature

David Foster, Editor

Arizona State University

TWAS 755

CLARICE LISPECTOR
(1925–1977)
Photograph courtesy of the
Carmen Balcells Agencia Literaria

Clarice Lispector

By Earl E. Fitz

The Pennsylvania State University

Twayne Publishers • Boston

Clarice Lispector

Earl E. Fitz

Copyright © 1985 by G.K. Hall & Company
All Rights Reserved
Published by Twayne Publishers
A Division of G. K. Hall & Co.
A publishing subsidiary of ITT
70 Lincoln Street
Boston, Massachusetts 02111

Book Production by Elizabeth Todesco
Book Design by Barbara Anderson

Printed on permanent/durable acid-free
paper and bound in the United States of
America.

Library of Congress Cataloging in Publication Data

Fitz, Earl E.
   Clarice Lispector.

   (Twayne's world author series; TWAS 755.   Latin American literature)
   Bibliography: p. 140
   Includes index
   1. Lispector, Clarice—Criticism and interpretation.
   I. Title.   II. Series: Twayne's world author series; TWAS 755.
   III. Series: Twayne's world author series.   Latin American literature.
PQ9697.L585Z66 1985   869.3   84-25199
   ISBN 0-8057-6605-7

Contents

About the Author

Earl E. Fitz is an associate professor of Portuguese, Spanish, and Comparative Literature at the Pennsylvania State University.

Preface

At the time of her death in 1977, Clarice Lispector was one of the most respected writers not only in Brazil but in Spanish America as well. Although she was never a "popular" author, in the sense that great numbers of people read her books, discerning readers throughout Latin America had praised her work for its brilliant use of language, its structural inventiveness, and its depiction of the alienated and frustrated modern human condition.

Owing, perhaps, to the strong philosophical bent of even her first work in 1944, Lispector's reputation as an introspective, lyrically expressive narrativist grew steadily and had, as early as 1954, also spread to Europe, in particular France and Germany, where she would eventually come to enjoy a substantial following. At times reminiscent of the French *nouveau roman,* and especially the novels of Nathalie Sarraute and Alain Robbe-Grillet, Lispector's own post–1949 fiction shows a constant concern over the way "things" in the physical world effect differing and often wholly unexpected responses in a person's consciousness.

As a writer, Lispector was less interested in events than in the repercussions these events produced in the minds of her characters, an approach to fiction writing that, in 1944, the year her first novel was published, put her largely at odds with what was then being done in the Brazilian novel and short story. Not surprisingly, then, very little "happens" in a typical Lispector tale; plot, if defined in terms of the traditional realistic novel, is virtually nonexistent. The conflict of the work is based, almost invariably, in the mind of the character most centrally involved, the character (like the "I" of a lyric poem) whose hermetic and at times even claustrophobic point of view dominates both the telling and the structuring of the story. More than anything else, Lispector's narratives, her novels and her shorter pieces, are philosophical and poetic exercises that probe the complex and shifting inner realities of modern men and women, especially women.

Her narratives blur the traditional distinctions between poetry and prose largely because of the ephemeral, idealistic material expressed in them and because of her own highly unique ideas about how this kind of material is best treated. Her novels, for example, up through *Um sopro de vida* (A breath of life; published posthumously in 1978), show themselves to be fully in accord, thematically, structurally, and stylistically, with what Ralph Freedman has described as the lyrical novel, the kind of novel written by Virginia Woolf (to whom Clarice Lispector has often been compared), Hermann Hesse (one of Lispector's favorite authors and one who, according to Lispector herself, had an important influence on her work), and André Gide.

More philosophical than these authors, however, Lispector labored tirelessly with ontological issues, in particular the question of human consciousness, with the nature of the relationship between language and reality and the human perception of both. Lispector's near obsessive concern over this sort of material imparted a very identifiable form, structure, and style to her work, making it one of the most easily recognized bodies of fiction in modern Brazilian literature. As one of her most astute critics once said, "no one writes like she does."

But while we can justifiably rank Clarice Lispector as one of Latin America's earliest and most successful "new novelists," she remains of special importance to Brazil. Within the confines of Brazilian literary history, Clarice Lispector will always be remembered for moving prose fiction away from the rote regionalism and doctrinaire social realism of the 1930s, for showing that there were other topics for Brazilian writers to discuss and that there were new ways to do it. When considered in this reformist context, Lispector shows her vital connection with the first generation of Brazil's modernist movement, a generation dominated by iconoclastic and highly experimental poetry as well as by a desire to be both international and nationalistic in theme and form.

By obliterating the (for her) specious and artificial distinctions that supposedly separated poetry and prose, Lispector freed herself from generic and thematic conventionality and in so doing paved the way for a near total concentration on language as both a medium of artistic and philosophic expression and as an object of inquiry itself. Always a phenomenologically inclined writer, Lispector created a new kind of prose fiction for Latin America, one that from her first novel onward focused on the mythopoeic, philosophical, and linguistic aspects of being and human consciousness. Like Joyce, from whom she borrowed the line that became the title of her first novel, Clarice Lispector was a writer who viewed language as the single most crucial factor in the creation of imaginative literature. As such, her work makes her both a precursor of the "new narrative" in Latin America and one of its most accomplished practitioners. Almost totally ignored in this important comparative context, Clarice Lispector's fiction has not yet received the critical attention that it merits.

This study, while undertaking certain intrinsic discussions of Lispector's work, will also attempt to place her in her proper Brazilian and Latin American context. It is hoped that the reader will not interpret her fiction as being an isolated case of narrative experimentalism in one of Western literature's most neglected national literatures, but as being that of an artist and thinker fully in tune with the intellectual and aesthetic trends of her time.

To accomplish this two-fold task, I will discuss certain internal aspects of Lispector's work—its style, structure, and point of view— while also commenting on the sundry external factors that have affected her career. The present study is not presented as a detailed and systematic analysis of all aspects of Clarice Lispector's fiction; it is intended as a general discussion of the most outstanding aspects of her work. No detailed and comprehensive study of Lispector's oeuvre, her novels, short stories, children's literature, translation work, essays, chronicles, and interviews, has as yet appeared in English. It is my hope that this present volume will begin to fill this lacuna and that it will help call attention to one of modern Latin America's most singular voices. Should this occur, then my work will have achieved its goal.

Earl E. Fitz

The Pennsylvania State University

Acknowledgments

The author would like to thank the following institutions for their generous help in the preparation of this manuscript: the Office of the Dean, College of Liberal Arts; the Liberal Arts Associate Dean for Research and Graduate Studies; the Institute for the Arts and Humanistic Studies; the Program in Comparative Literature; and the Department of Spanish, Italian, and Portuguese, all of the Pennsylvania State University.

A word of thanks must also go to David William Foster, Twayne's Latin American field editor, to the several people who helped in the typing of the manuscript, and especially to Gregory Rabassa, friend and mentor.

The author would like to thank the Carmen Balcells Literary Agency for permission to quote from the various Clarice Lispector texts, the Alfred A. Knopf publishing company for permission to quote from *The Passion According to G. H.,* the Center for Inter-American Relations for permission to quote from *Review 24,* and the University of Texas Press for permission to quote from *Family Ties.*

Special thanks, though, must go to my long-suffering wife, Julianne, and to our children, Ezra, Caitlin, and Dylan, all of whom paid many times over for the writing of this book.

Chronology

1925   Clarice Lispector born Tchetchelnik, the Ukraine, USSR, December 10 (because apparently no exact records were kept, the precise date remains in doubt).

1926   Family (father, mother, and three daughters) arrives in Alagoas, Brazil; Lispector two months old.

1929   Family moves to Recife, Pernambuco.

1931   Lispector learns to read; exhibits precocious interest in composing oral run-on tales for friends.

1932   Completes elementary schooling at the Grupo Escolar João Barbalho; begins to write simple stories, which she sends to local papers; none published.

1935   Begins secondary education at the Ginásio Pernambucano, in Recife.

1937   Family moves to the Tijuca section of Rio de Janeiro; Lispector reads such authors as Madame Delly, José de Alencar, Júlio Dinis, Monteiro Lobato, and Eça de Queirós; believes that books are born, like humans, not written; upon learning that people write books, Lispector decides that she, too, wants to become a writer; completes secondary studies at the Colégio Sílvio Leite, in Rio de Janeiro, and also publishes her first story.

1940   Begins studies at the Colégio Andrews; also begins to read such diverse authors as Machado de Assis, Graciliano Ramos, Jorge Amado, Mário de Andrade, Raquel de Queirós, Hermann Hesse, and Katherine Mansfield.

1941   Matriculates in the National Faculty of Law in Rio de Janeiro; takes job as editor at the Agência Nacional (a news agency); works with Antônio Callado and Lúcio Cardoso, the latter coming to have a significant influence on Lispector's early development as a writer; comes to know such experimental authors as Adonias Filho, Otávio de Faria, and Cornélio Pena; enters a volume of stories in a contest sponsored by José Olympio; Lispector does not win (the editors never received the stories) and later says that the pieces were both "very bad" and "immature" because she has not yet developed her own style.

1942   Secures a job as a reporter for *A Noite;* Cardoso, her colleague, suggests to her the title for a manuscript, *Perto do coração selvagem* (Close to the savage heart), on which she has been working; develops the habit of jotting down notes for her stories wherever and whenever they come to her; this process becomes her basic method of writing and would allow her to develop her distinctive voice.

1943   Marries a fellow law student, Mauri Gurgel Valente.

1944   Graduates with her husband from law school; likes criminal law but has no intention of practicing; *Perto do coração selvagem* wins Graça Aranha Prize; Lispector's husband enters the diplomatic corps and couple is posted to Naples, Italy; Lispector devotes all her time to the writing of a new novel, *O lustre* (The chandelier).

1946   Couple is sent to Berne, Switzerland; *O lustre;* discovers the fiction of Jean-Paul Sartre.

1949   Couple's first child, Pedro, born in Berne; Lispector returns to Brazil for a time; *A cidade sitiada.*

1952   *Alguns contos* (Some stories); lives six months in England before moving, with her husband, to United States.

1953   Second child, Paulo, born in Washington, D.C.

1954   *Perto do coração selvagem* published in France.

1959   Lispector and her husband separate; she returns to Rio de Janeiro with the children.

1960   *Laços de família (Family Ties).*

1961   *A maçã no escuro (The Apple in the Dark);* wins the Cármen Dolores Barbosa Prize.

1963   Lispector featured speaker at the Eleventh Congress of Iberoamerican Literature, Austin, Texas; argues that all true art is necessarily experimental in essence.

1964   *A legião estrangeira* (The foreign legion); *A paixão segundo G. H. (The Passion According to G. H.).*

1967   Begins, with *O mistério do coelho pensante* (The mystery of the thinking rabbit), to write children's literature; this first story wins a prize from the Campanha Nacional da Criança (National Children's Agency); suffers severe burns on right hand and both legs in an apartment fire; immobilized for several months.

1968   *A mulher que matou os peixes (The Woman Who Killed the Fish)*, another children's story.

1969   *Uma aprendizagem ou o livro dos prazeres* (An apprenticeship or the book of pleasures); wins the Golfinho de Ouro Prize.

1970   *A maçã no escuro* and *Laços de família* translated into German.

1971   *Felicidade clandestina* (Clandestine happiness).

1973   *Água viva (White Water); A imitação da rosa* (The imitation of the rose).

1974   *Onde estivestes de noite* (Where were you last night?); *A via crucis do corpo* (The via crucis of the flesh); *A vida íntima de Laura* (Laura's secret life); attends a convention at Cali, Colombia, and speaks on "The New Hispanoamerican Narrative"; Lispector's translation of *The Picture of Dorian Gray* published.

1975   *Visão do esplendor* (A vision of splendor); *De corpo inteiro* (Sound of body).

1976   Awarded first prize in the Tenth Concurso Literário Nacional (Tenth National Literary Competition) for her contribution to Brazilian literature; represents Brazil at the World Witchcraft Congress at Bogotá, Colombia; speaks on her story "O ôvo e a galinha" (The chicken and the egg).

1977   *A hora da estrela* (The time of the star); dies of cancer, December 9, in Rio de Janeiro, one day before her fifty-second birthday.

1978   Posthumous publication of *Para não esquecer* (In order not to forget); *Um sopro de vida: pulsações* (A breath of life: pulsations); *A bela e a fera* (Beauty and the beast); *Quase de verdade* (Almost true).

Chapter One
Biography and Background

The Formative Years

By the early 1920s Pedro and Marian Lispector had determined to leave Russia and emigrate to the Americas; the question was where, Brazil or the United States? Because late in 1925 there seemed to be too many obstacles involved in their coming to the United States, the family, consisting of the parents and two daughters (Tânia and Elisa), opted for Brazil. Departing their Ukranian homeland, the family set out for the Black Sea port of Odessa. But on the way a stop had to be made for the birth of a third daughter, Clarice, in Tchetchelnik, a village so small that it fails to appear on most maps of the region. Later in her life Lispector often said that the town meant nothing to her, except as a "fact" associated with her identity in an oddly disconnected and unrelated fashion.[1] She never returned to it.

Indeed, Lispector's existence before her arrival in Brazil never became an issue for her, at least insofar as her stories and novels were concerned. This is interesting because Lispector was sometimes faulted as a writer, especially during the 1940s, for not being "sufficiently Brazilian," for not writing a kind of fiction that could clearly be seen to relate directly to the sundry social, political, and cultural realities of Brazil at the time.[2] Even from the beginning, with *Perto do coração selvagem* (1944), Lispector's fictional world was perceived as being very different, singularly removed from what critics and readers had become accustomed to as "Brazilian literature." Thus it was, then, that Lispector's cultural identity began to take form when she was two months old, her age when she arrived early in 1926 with her family in the northeastern city of Alagoas. Soon afterwards, the family moved to Recife, where Lispector spent her childhood. By her own admission, Lispector's early years were happy ones, although later she would say she never realized how poor her family was.[3] She completed her elementary schooling at the Grupo Escolar João Barbalho and then began, in 1935, her secondary-school studies at the Ginásio Pernambucano. This work would be finished in 1937, at the Colégio Sílvio Leite, in Rio de Janeiro, where the family, seeking a more propitious financial situation, had moved.

The move to the more cosmopolitan Rio de Janeiro seems to have had decisive implications for Lispector's early intellectual development. Always a precocious child, Lispector responded quickly to the wealth of culture available to her in her new Rio setting. At age seven, having discovered that books were written by human beings (rather than being "born"), Lispector, perhaps already struck by the mystery of the creative act, resolved to become a writer herself. Although she had for some time made up stories for herself and her friends, she now, also at age seven, began to write simple stories that she then sent to the *Diário da tarde* in hopes of seeing them published. None ever was. Failing in her initial attempt to see her stories appear in print, Lispector, now a nine-year-old, composed a three-act play about "love." But this effort did not see the light of day, either, for the play's young author chose to keep it locked up in her bookcase rather than try to publish it.[4]

Influences

During these same early creative years, Lispector was a voracious reader. She was especially fond of Monteiro Lobato's *As reinações de Narizinho,* a book she read one page at a time so as to make it last as long as possible and which later appears in one of her stories, "Felicidade clandestina." She also read Madame Delly and Ardel, though she soon left these for such domestic masters as Graciliano Ramos, José de Alencar, and Machado de Assis, and such foreign writers as Eça de Queirós, Dostoyevski, Hesse, and Katherine Mansfield. Lispector often spoke of how, although she could not fully comprehend Dostoyevski, she was tremendously moved by him, especially his *Crime and Punishment.*[5] She has also indicated that Hesse's *Steppenwolf* had a great impact on her, as did many of the stories written by Katherine Mansfield, whom Lispector had discovered quite by accident one day while browsing in a Carioca bookshop. Lispector once said that she bought the Mansfield book because it looked interesting, she did not recognize the author, and she could afford it.[6]

Although it is always difficult to speak precisely about literary influence, it seems likely that in certain identifiable ways Dostoyevski, Hesse, and Mansfield each exerted a significant influence on the intellectual and artistic consciousness of the youthful Clarice Lispector. The intense, guilt-ridden psychological turmoil of *Crime and Punishment,* for example, would later emerge as a benchmark of Lispector's own mature fiction, as would the agonies of the fragmented personality so forcefully yet so beautifully expressed in *Steppenwolf.* It is also clear how the painful, hesitant, and often unsuccessful quest for a sense of personal identity so characteristic of such Mansfield stories as "The Garden-Party," "Bliss," and "Prelude" would later find echoes in Lispector's work.

And while it is often difficult if not impossible to prove cases of apparent literary influence, Lispector's response to the Mansfield pieces in particular seems surely to have been an event of great significance for her. One can only guess at what must have gone on in the young Brazilian writer's mind as she entered into the rarefied world inhabited by Mansfield's characters. In retrospect, we can see how both writers depended heavily not on logical analysis but on personal vision, on a kind of intuitive "knowing" or sentience about how things really are. Often, as in "The Tiredness of Rosabel" and "The Daydreams of a Drunk Woman" (*Family Ties,* Pontiero trans.), Mansfield's stories and Lispector's stories have a miraculous air about them, an eerie sense of mystery or "atmosphere," a curious, elusive, dreamlike quality, as if they were only partially connected to everyday reality. But even as they convey this delicate aura of thought and feeling, of susceptibility and acute sensitivity, Lispector and Mansfield never failed to anchor their ethereal stories in a very quotidian reality, the familiar things of daily life in the urban middle and upper-middle classes. While the former aspect is essentially thematic in nature, this latter feature of their fiction is conveyed stylistically through word choice and concrete description. Interestingly, both Mansfield and Lispector have been criticized for being weak at characterization and for drawing characters who lack substance or verisimilitude. One could respond to this criticism by answering that the short-story genre itself simply does not permit character development (as a novel does) and that, by way of contrast, the story form depends on showing how a moment or incident in the life of a character can reveal all there is to know about that character. Both Mansfield and Lispector wrote stories that turn on a sudden and powerfully dramatic flash of insight into a character's true nature. In response to the criticism that their characters are not "believable" or "lifelike," one might also say that Lispector and Mansfield were not primarily interested as writers in creating a realistically described world of objects and people in action; they were, in fact, more interested in another kind of reality, the emotive and psychological one of the mind and spirit, a reality composed of verbal nuance and suggestion and based on the inner experience of each character. Finally, the stories of Katherine Mansfield must have impressed Clarice Lispector with their cerebral tenor, their guarded wariness, their extreme subtlety of expression, their understated lyricism, their unsettling plots, and, perhaps most of all, their uncanny ability to make the most banal event speak volumes about a particular character's psychic condition. All these qualities began to emerge in Lispector's own work, a fact that, while not proving a case of literary influence, certainly gives us grounds for a fascinating comparative study.

The salient fact here is that the works of Dostoyevski, Hesse, and Mansfield, to say nothing of those of Machado de Assis, dealing as they do with the vicissitudes of the inner realm, seem to have struck a deep and responsive chord in Lispector's mind. Even as a nine-year-old girl, she was aware of being attracted to stories and characters of this type, stories that tended to eschew the world of physical action in favor of psychological portraiture and divagation. Lispector also became at this same time more conscious and selective of what she was reading and studying at school,[7] a fact that also suggests that while writers like Machado de Assis, Dostoyevski, Hesse, and Mansfield may not have directly determined the nature of her future as a writer, they must have deeply affected the girl's sensibilities. Lispector completed her secondary studies at the Colégio Sílvio Leite, Rio de Janeiro, in 1937, the same year that she decided she, too, wanted to become a writer.

The Making of a Writer

In 1940, having completed her studies at Andrews, Lispector matriculated in the National Faculty of Law, from which she graduated in 1944. It is often said that Lispector never had any intention of practicing law as a career and that in fact she entered law school primarily as a way of securing a more complete formal education. In later years Lispector would note that she was really interested in only a few of her courses, such as those dealing with criminal law and the lawyer's role in society, and that she actually completed her law degree in order to answer those of her colleagues who said she seldom finished what she started.[8] For three months Lispector also held a job as a legal secretary, but she did not find the work to her liking and soon left to work as a translator of scientific articles for a laboratory in the Botafogo district of Rio de Janeiro.

But Lispector left this job, too, after a short time and found a position that would have an important effect on her career as a writer. This post, that of an editor for the Agência Nacional, a news agency where she worked with such people as Antônio Callado, José Condé, and Lúcio Cardoso, returned Lispector to the intellectual's milieu, to a world made up of themes and ideas, of words and of concerns over such issues as form, style, and content. Cardoso, especially, had at this time a significant impact on Lispector's development as a writer. In this fecund environment, where she was constantly exposed to all aspects of the human experience, Lispector enjoyed herself at the same time that she began to think more and more seriously about writing as a vocation. She also began to gain valuable experience as an interviewer, an experience that in later years she would transform into fiction and build into her questioning, self-inquisitorial narratives. One of the most fascinating of these early interviews, and one that illuminates Lispector's own aesthetic and intellectual sensibility as much as her subject's, was with the renowned poet Augusto Federico Schmidt. In 1975 Lispector published *De corpo inteiro* (Sound of body), a collection of interviews she did with a variety of people in the arts, sciences, and humanities.

Later, in 1942, with her enthusiasm for writing thoroughly whetted by what had been an exhilarating experience at the Agência Nacional, Lispector transferred as a reporter to the paper *A noite*. Lispector was the only woman then working for the prestigious paper and, indeed, was one of Brazil's first woman journalists, a fact of which she was always very proud. This job also gave her an opportunity to experience firsthand some quite diverse people, issues, and ways of life, all of which served to give her the breadth she would later need to create her own stories and novels.

It was during this time, in fact, that Clarice Lispector actually began to compose her first novel, *Perto do coração selvagem* (Close to the savage heart), a work critiqued in manuscript form with great enthusiasm by Lispector's friend, colleague, and mentor, Lúcio Cardoso. Cardoso, himself an introspective and innovative author, recognized in Clarice Lispector a new writer of great potential and originality. Encouraging her and showing her how—and why—to refine her prose, Cardoso further suggested that Lispector take the title of her first manuscript from a line in Joyce's *A Portrait of the Artist as a Young Man.*

Other writers whose views on literature were important for Lispector at this time were Adonias Filho, Cornélio Pena, and Otávio de Faria, artists who were themselves members of an active literary circle centering around Tasso da Silveira. Within the confines of Brazilian literary history, then, one can say that by 1944 the time was ripe for a literary revolution. The only element lacking was the presence of a writer of sufficient originality, power, and imagination to bring it about. Clarice Lispector was that writer, a fact clearly borne out by the publication, in 1944, of *Perto do coração selvagem.*

The Works

Although the book was generally well received by the critics, with Sérgio Milliet declaring that it was "the most serious attempt at an introspective novel yet made in Brazil,"[9] it had been written "with much anguish" by its author.[10] Lispector said she "anguished" over it because "it followed her everywhere," with ideas about it coming to her at odd hours of the day and night and under inconvenient circumstances, such as when she was at the opera, walking down the street, at work, or in class.[11]

In an attempt to deal with the book's rather chaotic genesis, Lispector devised a method of writing that would, in time, become her standard method of composition, that of immediate annotation. Retiring early and arising around three or four in the morning, she would sit in her apartment drinking coffee, smoking, and thinking. She also liked to listen to music, both while she wrote and during those deeply private times of solitude and meditation. She once said, in fact, that she ruined her recording of Brahms's Fourth Symphony while working on *A maçã no escuro.*[12] Lispector also carried a notebook with her wherever she went and would jot down scraps of dialogue, ideas, and notes about characters, scenes, and themes as they came to her. Describing the way she worked, Lispector once said, "Sometimes everything starts with just one word. A word will suddenly wake me up and then I'll write a sentence. I take notes upon notes, file them away, and then comes the terrible job of mounting them into some kind of meaningful structure. That's when I get terribly lazy. For me, the most interesting part is taking notes."[13] This process explains part—but, as we shall see, not all—of Lispector's unmistakable style, a style that has been praised by Milliet, Cardoso, Rabassa, and others for its spontaneity, its rich and powerful imagery, and for its unusual syntax. Because Lispector had expressed some concern about the overall unity and cohesion her work would have given this method of writing, Cardoso once assured her that as long as all her notes addressed themselves somehow to the same subject, they would ultimately fall into place and impart an inner unity to the finished work.[14]

Since this became Lispector's basic method of composition, it is surprising to note that she did not typically labor over her prose, Flaubert-like, once it had reached its "final form." Her explanation was that in annotating her notes, something she did assiduously, she automatically reworked them, stylistically and structually, into the form they would finally have in print.[15] For a writer whose style is as unique as Lispector's, such an explanation of how she came to create her pieces inspires as many questions as it answers. When once asked, in fact, about how she had developed such a distinctive style, Lispector responded that she did not know any other way to write and that this was simply how she did it,[16] implying that her own creative process was largely a mystery for her as well as for her readers.[17] However arrived at, Lispector's style is quite distinctive; her work resembles no one else's, a fact not lost on those Brazilian critics of the 1940s who were receptive to stylistic experimentation and innovation.

After marrying a classmate, Mauri Gurgel Valente, in 1943, and graduating from law school the following year, Lispector accompanied her diplomat husband to Naples, Italy, where he had been posted. Once there, she began work on her second novel, *O lustre* (The chandelier), after first serving for a time as an aide in a hospital for wounded Brazilian soldiers. Although her first work, *Perto do coração selvagem,* had won the Graça Aranha prize, Lispector did not yet consider herself a professional writer; rather, she saw herself as an "amateur" (an *escritora amadora*),[18] as a woman who wrote because she loved writing passionately, because she felt she had to. Lispector often alluded to the compulsiveness of her approach to fiction writing, to her intense, deeply personal need to perform the physical, often (for her) cathartic act of writing. Reflecting this personal intensity of the author, *O lustre* follows closely the thematic, sylistic, and structural pattern established in the first novel. In this second effort, however, Lispector had already begun to refine her art, employing a more complex symbolism and focusing more sharply on the development of a specific character's individual sense of identity, one tied closely to the themes of death and decay and the social problems connected with the issues of sexual, social, and psychological domination.

In the same year, 1946, that *O lustre* was published to a predominantly positive critical response, Lispector and her husband moved to Berne, Switzerland. Three years later Lispector gave birth to her first son, Pedro, and saw her third novel published. This work, the ironic, metaphoric *A cidade sitiada* (The besieged city), took Lispector the longest time to write, perhaps because it undertook an interior search for something the author herself had not yet defined.[19] Similar in many ways to the two novels that preceded it, *A cidade sitiada* was different in that it placed increased significance on the role environment plays in the development of the mind that perceives it. Although concerned more extensively with an exterior world than were the first two novels, *A cidade sitiada* is nevertheless held together, as the first two works were, by the silent, though powerful, inner reflections of its protagonist.

Although her duties as a mother took up most of her time during the late 1940s and early 1950s, Lispector still found time to write. Thinking, as a parent does, about trying to do several things at once, she even devised a method of writing while taking care of her son: by resting her typewriter on her lap, Lispector found she could work while still sitting close enough to her infant son to look after him. Like her system of annotated note taking and her early morning arising, this habit of typewriting with the machine sitting on her knees also became something of a habit with Lispector, another of her creative idiosyncrasies.

By 1951 Lispector had also begun to turn her attention to the challenging short-story form, dropping for a time her efforts at extended narrative. The clarity of Lispector's vision and her ability to focus intensely on the most intimate or ephemeral aspects of her subject made the short story an ideal vehicle for her talents as a writer. With the publication of *Alguns contos* (Some stories) in 1952 Lispector immediately established herself as a powerful new force in Brazilian short fiction. As many critics have noted, Lispector, in fact, may well have done her best work in the story form. Her reputation as a technically demanding author rests largely, and with considerable justification, on her skills as a story writer rather than on her prowess as a novelist. Her novels, though often outstanding achievements in their own right, can seem diffuse and digressive in contrast to the tightly structured stories. Thematically, however, the pieces included in *Alguns contos* are cut from the same cloth as the earlier novels. We see the same penchant for psychological portraiture rather than action, the same lyrical ambience, and the same phenomenological connections between a person's mercurial inner world and the mysterious outer world that surrounds him.

The next few years show an abatement in Lispector's literary endeavors. The ever-increasing demands of family life, simple fatigue, and the complexities of being married to a diplomat precluded Lispector's writing as much as she might have. The family traveled a great deal as well, moving from Berne to England, for six months, and then on to Washington, D.C. Lispector resided in Washington for seven years and bore her second son, Paulo, there as well. In spite of all the other demands on her time and energy, however, Lispector had not during these years given up completely on her writing. Indeed, the notes for her next work, the long and complex novel, *A maçã no escuro (The Apple in the Dark)*, had actually been made before Lispector arrived in the United States. Additionally, Lispector, true to form, was busily compiling notes for yet another work, one that would become a second and even more successful collection of short stories, *Laços de família (Family Ties)*. Deftly transforming some of these annotated compilations of ideas, themes, and characters into short fictions, Lispector published a few of them in the magazine *Senhor* (Gentleman). One of these pieces, "O crime do professor de matemática," ("The Crime of the Mathematics Professor"), would eventually become one of Lispector's most famous tales. Translated into English, it later appeared in the American journal *Odyssey*.

The novel in gestation at this same time, *A maçã no escuro,* proved more difficult to complete than had the stories she was working on. Revised eleven times, with the first manuscript running five hundred pages,[20] *A maçã no escuro,* in its final form, stands out as a decisive moment in Lispector's growth as a novelist. Representing the high point of her career up to that time,[21] this symbolic, introspective, and searching book shows Lispector embracing many of the narrative techniques that we associate with the mature work of such writers as Woolf, Hesse, and Gide. Although there is no solid evidence that Lispector consciously strove to develop a specific kind of novel writing or to emulate anyone else's style, it is known, as noted earlier, that she had been impressed by Hesse's *Steppenwolf*. It is reasonable, then, to assume that this latter novel, thoroughly poetic in both form and content,[22] exerted a significant influence on Lispector's own ideas about the nature of her own work. In any event, *A maçã no escuro* is clearly the culmination of the kind of philosophical and introspective writing that Lispector had been doing up to 1961.[23] Her work after this prize-winning novel, which was given an impeccable English translation by the renowned translator Gregory Rabassa in 1967, shows itself to be more and more typical of what Ralph Freedman has termed the lyrical novel.[24] As evidenced by *A maçã no escuro* and some of her later works, this kind of writing would help place Brazilian fiction on a par with the revolution in narrative that was sweeping through Spanish America, a revolution that would become known as the "Boom" in Spanish American literature.

Fully expressive of this technical revolution, *A maçã no escuro* also shows a primary concern with the relationship between language and reality, how one invents or controls the other, and with the ontological problems connected with our sense of being, our identity. These two issues, which are easily discernible in Lispector's earlier works, become, in *A maçã no escuro*, integral elements in the novel's basic structuring. Lispector succeeds here, in a way she had failed to do in the first three novels, in thoroughly unifying her content with her form, in making one inseparable from the other. In short, *A maçã no escuro* has the kind of organic unity that we expect in the well-crafted novel.

The close attention paid to a unification of the linguistic and philosophical concerns, then, is what sets *A maçã no escuro* apart from Lispector's pre-1961 attempts and what makes it one of the most important novels of the 1960s in Latin America. In subsequent novels, these same two concerns would recur constantly, finally becoming defining characteristics of Lispector's mature fiction.

Termed "one of the most important works of Brazilian fiction of any era,"[25] *A maçã no escuro* will be remembered for at least two reasons: it succeeded in establishing for Brazilian literature a new mode of fiction writing, the self-consciously introspective language novel, and it proved that Brazilian narrative could be as sophisticated as any being written anywhere in the Western tradition. In this dual function, then, *A maçã no escuro* represents both an artistic success and a cultural breakthrough. In the person of Clarice Lispector, Brazilian literature had produced a writer who, without relying on servile reworkings of imported forms or themes, was producing original and striking works of fiction that were comparable with any on the then current international scene. That this significant event even took place is, as Gregory Rabassa has observed,[26] less a factor of foreign influence than a question of a talented and imaginative artist responding to the aesthetic and philosophical ethos of an age.

After three years of intense labor, Lispector saw two more remarkable books published, books that expand on themes first addressed in *A maçã no escuro* but that also break some new technical and thematic ground for their author. *A legião estrangeira* (1964; The foreign legion) and *A paixão segundo G. H.* (1964; *The Passion According to G. H.*) were greeted enthusiastically by the critics, who were quick to note and applaud the new developments in Lispector's themes and techniques.

A legião estrangeira, a collection of stories and chronicles, contains not only some of Lispector's best short pieces, such as "Os desastres de Sofia" ("Sofia's Disasters"), "O ôvo e a galinha" (The chicken and the egg), and "A quinta história" (The fifth story), but also some illuminating statements about Lispector's poetics, about how and why she writes as she does. Several of the nonfiction pieces included in the "No fundo de gaveta" section are particularly useful in understanding Lispector's thoughts about what literature is and what is involved, for her, in writing it.[27] Of these pieces, "O segrêdo" (The secret), "Aventura" (Adventure), "Escrever, prolongar o tempo" (Writing and the prolongation of time), "Dois modos" (Two ways), "Submissão ao processo" (Submission to the process), "Escrever, humildade, técnica" (Writing humility and technique), and "A explicação inútil" (The useless explanation) all strongly suggest how the concepts of intuition, process, time, fluidity, flux, and silence are of central importance in regard to Lispector's deeply personal approach to writing.

The other work published in 1964, *A paixão segundo G. H.*, is a profoundly speculative novel, one reminiscent in theme and structure of Sartre's *La nausée* (1938) and Virginia Woolf's *The Waves*

(1931). Stylistically poetic while thematically philosophic, *A paixão
segundo G. H.* gives credence to the notion that at their highest
levels of expression poetry and philosophy merge, that they show
themselves to be motivated by a similar desire for truth and accuracy
of expression. As suggested in its title, this hermetic fifth novel
works with the concept of "passion" in both its Christian context,
which alludes to Christ, and its Greek context, which means "to
suffer."[28] This results in a strikingly paradoxical situation, one in
which Lispector, a writer of Jewish heritage, uses a fundamentally
Christian religious language to convey what amounts to a basically
profane view of the world.[29]

Although some readers have felt that the philosophical aspects of
this work overshadowed its fictional features, most have found it
the powerful and moving record of a human mind locked in the
painful and unsettling process of self-discovery, of confrontation
with the truth about one's self and one's universe. In this sense, its
preoccupation with the spiritual transformation wrought in a person
who moves from a condition of ignorance to one of awareness, the
reader sees how *A paixão segundo G. H.* is a distillation and an
intensification of a similar experience undergone by Martim, the
focal-point character of *A maçã no escuro,* Virgínia of *O lustre,* and
Lucrécia Neves of *A cidade sitiada.*

In a more general way, however, it can also be said to represent
the culmination of what had been happening to Lispector's protagonists ever since the awakening of Joana in *Perto do coração selvagem.*
It is interesting to note that, while told essentially the same story
in these works (though with variations in treatment and new material
being constantly added), the reader who is sensitive to the special
attributes of the lyrical novel does not tire of reading them. This
is true for two reasons: first, Lispector's technique, her mode of
expression, was both a challenge to and a reward for the careful
reader. Like the best of modern poetry, Lispector's prose is charged
with paradox, internal rhythms, nuance, hidden connections, and
entrancing ambiguities. The case of Clarice Lispector is that of the
writer whose manner of telling the tale is sometimes more capti-
vating than the tale that is told, especially when one suspects that
the same story had been told, though in a different fashion, in an
earlier work. The second reason for Lispector's growing success was
that she, perhaps more than any other writer of her generation,
succeeded in tapping the mythopoetic roots of the human condi-

tion.[30] As is true of her brilliant predecessor Machado de Assis, Lispector was a writer whose basic theme was not Brazil or Brazilians but the human condition. A visionary, questioning writer, Lispector relied heavily on archetypal and mythic themes and forms to take her fiction deeply into the most hidden recesses of the human spirit. By constructing her fiction, consciously or unconsciously, around certain motifs (e.g., darkness, the instant, and silence) and archtypal patterns (the quest), Lispector was able to transcend the regional and achieve statements of universal significance.

In 1967 Lispector's son Paulo asked her why she had never written anything for children. She responded by composing *O mistério do coelho pensante* (The mystery of the thinking rabbit), which was the first of four tales she would write for children. Always fond of children and seriously attentive to what she regarded as their typically uninhibited and therefore revealing comments, Lispector later wrote three additional works of children's literature: *A mulher que matou os peixes* (1969; *The Woman Who Killed the Fish*), *A vida íntima de Laura* (1974; Laura's secret life), and *Quase de verdade* (1978; Almost true). Like *Le Petit Prince*, Lispector's "children's stories" are really as much for adults as for children.[31] Indeed, in reading these stories one realizes that their fablelike tone is achieved largely because Lispector treats them not as simple tales for unsophisticated readers—that is, children—but as highly distilled but unambiguously presented versions of the narratives she had written for her adult readers. Read on one level, for example, *A mulher que matou os peixes* is about how a very busy lady forgot to feed some fish.[32] The result was that they died. But on another level, the story is about guilt and its expiation, precisely the dominating theme of Lispector's famous short story "O crime do professor de matemática." So strong is the sense of guilt in the curiously eerie "children's story," one full of the muted violence and terror Lispector sees everywhere, that a child of ten wrote to her saying, "It's not your fault. You didn't do it on purpose. It's just that you were busy with other important things and you forgot to feed the fish."[33] When considering Lispector's children's stories in the light of her other work, it becomes clear why she considered children "primitive beings": they are often more honest, direct, and open in their personal and public dealings than are adults. Lispector also viewed animals as primitive beings, but as "a force of nature" that "confront our own animality."[34] Unlike children, they do not possess the human ability to reason and express themselves through speech, that most complex and perhaps most maddening of all our gifts.

Also in 1967 Lispector suffered severe burns in an apartment fire that was caused, authorities believed, when a lighted cigarette was accidentally dropped into some bedclothes. Suffering great pain because of her injuries, Lispector underwent skin graft surgery to correct the damage done to her hands and legs. After recovering from this ordeal, Lispector began to write in earnest once again. Supporting herself as a full-time and now widely recognized writer, Lispector branched out into such nonfiction and tangentially related forms as the chronicle. She also wrote a weekly column for the prestigious *Jornal do Brasil* (Journal of Brazil), did interviews in the magazines *Manchete* (Headline) and *Fatos e fotos* (Facts and photos), and undertook translations.

It was also during this difficult time that Lispector's reputation as something of a reclusive, occasionally "difficult" person began to take on proportions that were not, in fact, justified. She was occasionally portrayed by some of her detractors as being, for example, indifferent to Brazil's social and political problems. The truth, however, is that, as in the case of Borges, Clarice Lispector's art demands consideration on grounds other than overtly sociopolitical ones. Lispector's fiction is of the kind that requires us to maintain a clear distinction between an author who is politically aware and the sometimes apolitical art produced by that author.

Clarice Lispector was a strong-willed, highly intelligent woman, one who struggled to develop as fully as possible as a human being and a writer. Her fiction makes it clear that she was an intellectual and an artist who constantly strove to penetrate what, for her, was the enigma of the human experience. She wanted always to seize the core of things, to understand, and, finally, to show others so that they might too "see" the ultimate, ineffable truths about the human condition. Her work is a testimony to a writer whose burning impulse was to express the unexpressible, to say what cannot be said, to speak, as Wittgenstein suggested in his *Philosophical Investigations,* of that which we cannot speak, to do battle with those aspects of the human experience that defy linguistic control. Consciously committed to this paradoxical struggle, Lispector had little time for social or intellectual sham, triviality, or dishonesty, all of which were by-products of the active literary milieu that Brazil was enjoying during the turbulent 1960s. Although she always considered herself a politically "aware" writer,[35] she lived an increasingly withdrawn life in her Leme apartment, residing there with a companion nurse, Ciléia Marchi, a housekeeper, and her inseparable companion, a dachshund named Ulisses (who narrates the story in *Quase de verdade*).

In 1969 Lispector returned to the writing of extended narrative with *Uma aprendizagem ou o livro dos prazeres* (An apprenticeship, or the book of pleasures),[36] a novel that has not yet received the critical attention it deserves. Although once again dealing with the theme of self-discovery, and therefore consistent in a limited way with what Lispector had done previously, *Uma aprendizagem* was unique for two reasons: it was structured around not one person but two, and its socially relevant theme was developed more through the extensive use of meaningful dialogue, something that Lispector had not done up to the creation of this novel. The two primary characters, a young man and woman, come to know themselves only by reaching out, intellectually and emotionally, to touch each other. Considered by many to be Lispector's "strangest" novel, *Uma aprendizagem* is Lispector's first statement about how a person trapped in the essential solitude of human existence might attempt to break out, to get beyond the solipsism of one's own being and find some way of mitigating the basic isolation, that ironically, we all share as human beings. The couple's struggle to establish a secure and legitimate sense of identity, which, when finally achieved, allows them to accept the imperfections inherent in human relationships, provides the primary focus of the story. *Uma aprendizagem* is a challenging work, stylistically and structurally, with its beginning and end recalling Joyce's *Finnegans Wake,* for example, but it also numbers among Lispector's most human and optimistic works.

During this time Lispector continued to write stories. In 1971, for example, she published *Felicidade clandestina* (Clandestine happiness), a collection of short narratives that once again gave evidence of an author who was faithful to her old themes but who was ever innovative in regard to style, tone, and setting. Of the twenty-five pieces that comprise this collection, however, only nine had not been previously published. The new stories continued the entrancing ambiguity and paradox of Lispector's earlier efforts, but they sometimes lacked the emotional and intellectual intensity of the earlier pieces, especially those of *Laços de família,* which must be considered one of the best story collections in modern Latin American literature.

The new element present in the laconic tales of *Felicidade clandestina* was an understated, subtly expressed ironic tone, which was less comic or biting than resigned and wryly capitulative in the face of what the author depicts as the fundamental mystery of much, if not all, human behavior. Two stories, "Duas histórias a meu modo" (Two stories my way) and "O primeiro beijo" (The first kiss), bear this out, with the former piece also showing a new self-consciousness on the part of Lispector's narrators, a technical feature she would exploit in such later works as *A hora da estrela* and *Um sopro de vida*.

During part of this same period Lispector was again making notes for another, longer work, one that would ultimately take nearly three years to complete. This work, a sparely written but intensely poetic "fiction" in monologue, was *Água viva (White Water)*.[37] Derived from personal experience and termed a "fiction" by Lispector herself,[38] *Água viva* seemingly calls on one level for an autobiographical reading. Yet on another, more objective level it is a beautiful and deeply moving statement about love and freedom, about how a loving relationship cannot exist between people unless each party not only accepts but actively encourages the growth and development of the other. Love between human beings cannot exist, *Água viva* tells us, when one person is the master and the other is the slave. With a sense of paradox that is characteristic of the mature Clarice Lispector, *Água viva* suggests that love, that most total of surrenders, is achieved only in a state of total freedom and complete self-realization. In this sense, *Água viva,* a brilliant achievement in its own right and one of the most critically neglected Latin American novels of the 1970s, can be seen as an extension of and variation on *Uma aprendizagem ou o livro dos prazeres.* As a lyrical novel, *Água viva* is a tour de force, a work that reveals Lispector's creative powers in this particular genre. More than any of Lispector's other novels, *Água viva* succeeds in establishing an organic union between its form (a series of metaphorically expressed "time instants" arranged in certain interlocking patterns) and its content (the story of a woman who literally re-creates herself by writing the very narrative we are reading). Also published in 1973 is *A imitação da rosa* (The imitation of the rose), a new edition of some of Lispector's previously published and most popular stories.

The following year, 1974, Lispector brought out two additional collections of new stories and short narratives, *Onde estivestes de noite* (Where were you last night) and *A via crucis do corpo* (The via crucis of the flesh). While these two books contain much that is vintage Clarice Lispector, they also continue with the same wry yet pathetic irony that had appeared in *Felicidade clandestina*. A certain kind of humor (an aspect of Lispector's fiction that has been largely over-looked) begins to appear in these two books. More suggestive than expressed, this humor is present in a sporadic and unexpected fash-ion, but it archly merges Lispector's penchant for chronicling an anguished and tragically isolated inner drama with the wholly un-comprehending superficiality of most human intercourse. Basically, Lispector's sense of humor grimly reflects a narrative self-conscious-ness at how the world is simultaneously tragic and absurd. *A via crucis do corpo,* moreover, is perhaps the most direct of Lispector's post-1969 fiction, the work in which she involves the reader most openly in the "creation of the text," of its "content" and of its "significance." It is also notable for its frank carnality, with many of the stories dealing in whole or in part with overtly sexual aspects of being.

1975 saw the publication of *Visão do esplendor* (Vision of splendor) and *De corpo inteiro* (Sound of body), nonfiction works composed of chronicles, essays of a reflective nature, and interviews. Three of the essays from *Visão do esplendor,* "Explicação para quem talvez não entenda" (An essay for anyone who might not understand), "O 'verdadeiro' romance" (The "true" novel), and "Perguntas e respostas para um caderno escolar" (Questions and answers for a student note-book), are, along with "No fundo de gaveta" *(Legião estrangeira),* further statements by Lispector herself about her views on literature and writing. Another essay, also from *Visão do esplendor,* "O primeiro livro de cada uma de minhas vidas" (The first book of each of my lives), tells how, as a young girl of thirteen and fifteen, Lispector responded to a discovery of Hermann Hesse and Katherine Mans-field. *O Lobo da Estepe (Steppenwolf)* fascinated Lispector, we learn, with its hermetic, interiorized tale about the warring aspects of the human spirit, while Mansfield's searching, delicate stories caused Lispector to identify in a personal way with her vision of the world.

"Official" recognition of Clarice Lispector came in 1976 when she was cited by the Fundação Cultural do Distrito Federal for her outstanding contributions to Brazilian literature. Effectively en-shrining Lispector in the history of arts and letters in Brazil, the granting of this award attested to the fact that she had exerted a positive, renovating force on the writing of literature in Brazil.

Although it has often been suggested that, like Virginia Woolf, Proust, or Joyce, Clarice Lispector was a writer more talked about than read, by the late 1970s her presence was felt by the public and critics alike. By 1976 Lispector had become a major writer not only in Brazil but in the rest of Latin America as well, and the awarding of the Cultural Foundation Prize was recognition of this fact.

But Lispector, who wrote not to create "great art" but to satisfy a deeply felt impulse, did not rest on her laurels. To the contrary, with *A hora da estrela* (1977; The time of the star) she completed a novel that, structurally, represented a significant change from what she had previously done. Though still concerned with the process by which a human being realizes his or her private and public self, Lispector undertook in this novel a discussion of one of Brazil's most chronic and pressing social problems: the forced migration of people from the poverty-ridden Northeast to the overcrowded and over-burdened industrial centers of the South. Although not entirely successful in its very conscious effort to join together a lyrically (and ironically) presented realization of self with a strong, socially ori-ented statement about how life in the Northeast cripples the emo-tional and intellectual growth of its people, *A hora da estrela* is an important work because it proves, as if proof were needed, that Lispector was both aware of and concerned about modern Brazil's social ills. Additionally it suggests that Lispector was not a one-dimensional author, that she could vary her material. Had she not died at such an early age, Clarice Lispector might well have shown us new ways to make literature a positive force for social change.

Composed concurrently with *A hora da estrela*, *Um sopro de vida* (A breath of life) was published posthumously in 1978. More con-sistently poetic than any of Lispector's earlier works, with the pos-sible exception of *Água viva*, and written in the confessional mode, *Um sopro de vida* is the final statement about life, death, art, and being by an author who knew she was dying of a terminal disease. Though uneven in its style and irregular in its structure, the book nevertheless offers us a glimpse of how a courageous and honest intellect comes to grips with the reality of impending death.

Another posthumous work, and one that is of unusual value for those interested in assessing Lispector's development as a short-story writer, is *A bela e a fera* (1979; Beauty and the beast). This book, a compilation of the first stories Lispector ever wrote plus the last two she wrote, is immensely useful in attempting to evaluate her artistic evolution as a narrativist.

Not feeling well, Lispector went to the doctor on November 1, 1977, for a check-up. The diagnosis was cancer, which had already spread beyond the capacity of drugs and therapy to control it. Realizing fully what this meant, Lispector entered the hospital on November 16 for what she knew would be a futile struggle against death. She died on December 9, 1977, one day before her fifty-second birthday. She had wanted to be buried in São João Batista cemetery because, as she is reported to have said, "It's closer; people can come visit me."[39] But this was not to be. Clarice Lispector was laid to rest on December 11, 1977, in the Cemitério Comunal Israelita, Caju, Rio de Janeiro.[40]

Chapter Two

The Place of
Clarice Lispector
in the History of
Brazilian Literature

In order to appreciate the historical importance of Lispector's work, we must place it in its proper perspective. This means that we must interpret it as forming part of a national literary tradition as well as representing certain international trends and developments regarding the nature of narrative. Seen as a Brazilian writer, Clarice Lispector appears to be something of an anomaly, a writer whose work does not typically reflect the Jorge Amado-like regionalism for which Brazilian literature has long been famous. Indeed, Lispector's general disinclination to write fiction that is socially "committed" in the orthodox sense of this term has caused some problems in terms of her reception by certain critics and readers. This was especially true during the first few years of her career, when she was struggling to establish herself as a writer and to find her true voice. That she was not overtly political in her work should not be taken to mean, however, that Lispector lacked a social conscience, for she did not.[1] To the contrary, during the whole of her life she was an ardent champion of social justice and equality in Brazil. Having grown up in what might be termed a "disadvantaged," not to say "poor," home environment, Lispector gained firsthand knowledge about the inequalities that plague Brazilian society. And as a woman, she quickly learned of another pernicious kind of discrimination, one that would, in its own fashion, find its way thematically into nearly all of her fiction. In law school, an intellectually maturing Lispector exhibited a keen interest in those subjects which dealt with the role of law in bringing about a more equitable and just social structure for Brazil. Throughout her life Clarice Lispector was acutely aware of social issues, and while her fiction is not socially oriented in any obvious sense, as in the manner of Jorge Amado, Raquel de Queirós, Graciliano Ramos, or José Lins do Rêgo, neither is it devoid of social relevance.

One could say, in fact, that as an urban writer for whom "social inter-relationships are the very fabric of her fiction,"[2] Lispector is very much a socially relevant writer. Moreover, in her capacity as interpreter of the twentieth-century urban consciousness, Clarice Lispector has been a pioneer in dissecting the psychological state of Brazilian men and women.[3] Within this thematic orientation no one in Brazilian narrative has surpassed her in plumbing the depths of the modern woman's sense of self and her role in society. Although Lispector's handling of this basically feminist subject matter is challenging in terms of what she demands of the reader, it is one indication of how Clarice Lispector succeeded in internationalizing and deparochializing Brazilian literature in the second half of the twentieth century. This renovating spirit is the link that connects Lispector to the thrust of the Modernist revolt that began for Brazil in February 1922.

Modernism in Brazil

The Modernists, led in theory and often in practice by Mário de Andrade and Oswald de Andrade, sought to free Brazilian art from what they felt were outdated or artificial forms, themes, and modes of expression. To achieve this aesthetic liberation they availed themselves of several avant-garde movements from post–World War I Europe, such as Primitivism, Futurism, Expressionism, and Dadaism. The Brazilian Modernists, as Claude Hulet has shown, were also keenly interested in such new literary forms as free verse, the *roman fleuve,* and the Anglo-American multilevel novel.[4] At the same time, however, Brazil's early Modernists began searching for authentic "Brazilianisms," for themes and characters that were indigenous in nature and not importations of foreign material. The somewhat paradoxical thrust of this immensely significant urge to be cosmopolitan as well as nationalistic led the Modernists to combine nativist subject matter with certain new foreign themes and forms. The results, while always interesting, were also occasionally incongruous.

But the two key principles, the "cosmopolitan" urge to bring Brazilian letters into the mainstream of Western culture and the "nationalistic" urge to create an authentic Brazilian literature, one based truly on national themes, forms, and modes of expression,[5] were sound. There were three main stages, or movements, to the Modernist revolt in Brazil:[6] stage 1 (1920–1930) was dominated by inconoclastic poetry and concerned thematically with advocating Brazil's cultural independence; stage 2 (1930–1945) was dominated by prose fiction, especially the "Novel of the Northeast" (Jorge Amado, Graciliano Ramos, Raquel de Queirós, and José Lins do Rêgo, principally),[7] and was strongly committed to social justice and national development. Stage 2, which encompasses one of modern Brazil's most turbulent political eras, was dominated by the charismatic figure of Getúlio Vargas, who dictatorially ruled Brazil from 1930 to 1945 and again from 1950 to 1954. Stage 2 was also the period when Lispector wrote and published her first novel. Stage 3 (1945–1960) was marked by a growth in criticism and the essay. This latter form, reflecting a healthy spirit of self-scrutiny, focused on such diverse fields as political science, sociology, anthropology, and economics as well as on literature and the fine arts. There was no dearth of high quality literature during stage 3, however, as poetry and prose both saw some great works produced. During this time Carlos Drummond de Andrade, Manuel Bandeira, and Cecília Meireles were at or near the peak of their creative powers, as were João Cabral de Melo Neto, Jorge Amado, Guimarães Rosa, and Clarice Lispector. Literarily it was a very fecund period, with several prose writers, notably Rosa and Lispector, producing some of their finest, most original, and lasting work.[8] It is here, then, in the rebellious and reformist context of Brazilian Modernism, that we should begin to assess Lispector's development as a writer.

Seen from this national perspective, her *Perto do coração selvagem* (1944) was as radically different, structurally and thematically, from the documentary realism of the 1930s as Mário de Andrade's *Macunaíma* (1928) or Oswald de Andrade's *As memórias sentimentais de João Miramar* (1924; the sentimental memoirs of João Miramar), or his later *Seraphim ponte grande* (1933; *Seraphim Grosse Pointe*), were to the staid, rather unimaginative and derivative prose fiction of the first decade of the twentieth century. Exceptions, of course, would include the extraordinary case of Machado de Assis and much of the work of Graça Aranha and Lima Barreto. Similar to *Macunaíma* and the two Cubist-like works by Oswald de Andrade, Lispector's first novel was controversial because of the interiorized themes it undertook to explore and the technical and stylistic innovations it employed. And while such works as *Macunaíma, As memórias sentimentais de João Miramar,* and *Seraphim ponte grande* have a certain external frivolity about them, this really masks a much more serious concern: how does a writer express the truth about human reality without falling prey to dead language and to outmoded themes and forms? Though deeply involved with essentially the same issue, Lispector's novel offers the reader no whimsy or facade behind which he can seek refuge from the demands the work makes upon him. Involving the reader directly in the creation of the text's significance, *Perto do coração selvagem* is a serious work written about a serious subject—the psychological anxiety that befalls a person (in this case a young woman) who attempts to reject false modes of existence and embrace authentic ones. Though not apparent at the time of its publication (1944), this essentially feminist theme had a preeminently relevant social value. It is important to note in this regard, however, that while (as we shall see) Lispector was not comfortable in describing herself and her work as "feminist," her fiction tends overwhelmingly to focus on the psychic and social existences of modern urban women. With this novel, then, Lispector established herself as one of Latin America's pioneer feminists (in the spirit if not the letter of the term) as well as one of its very first "new novelists."

Just as the Modernists sought to reject a spurious and often artificially attained sense of national identity, Lispector, as a post–World War II or stage 3 Modernist, sought to call attention to the despair, frustration, and angst that derive from the attempt of people, especially middle-class urban women, to live out a life based on materialism, self-delusion, and dependency. Lispector does not openly attack these bourgeoisie for being what they are, socially or politically, for in truth we hardly know them in these contexts. As we see in *Perto do coração selvagem,* Lispector does not "attack" them at all; in fact she allows them to show the reader, through their words, deeds, and dealings with other people, just how vacuous they are, how shallow and inauthentic are their lives. Yet we do not loathe these often pathetic creatures, for, like Joana and Otávio *(Perto do coração selvagem),* their lives are reflections of our lives. Psychologically and culturally, we understand them all too well, and this is the source of the unique kind of verisimilitude that Lispector's best characters possess. Sometimes, when they confront themselves honestly and openly, they realize, if even but for a moment, what they should do, what course of action would make them more authentic beings. The problem, as Lispector's characters intuitively sense (if not necessarily understand), is how to cope with the sense of dislocaton that this all but unbearable burden produces in them. In a very human sense, then, the novels of the Andrades and Clarice Lispector all confront the issue of authenticity of being: one *(Macunaíma)* is openly nationalist in context; two others *(As memórias sentimentais de João Miramar* and *Serafim ponte grande)* partially personalize the issue; and one *(Perto do coração selvagem)* not only renders it a totally personalized vision, but a metaphor for existence as well.

Beyond their formal parallels and their concern over how a writer presents the truth, the novels and stories of Clarice Lispector and the three other chief Modernist novels noted exhibit a third similarity, their mythopoetic moorings. Like much of Brazil's stage 2 Modernist poetry, such as Cassiano Ricardo's *Martim Cererê* (1928) or Raul Bopp's *Cobra Norato* (1928), Clarice Lispector's ceaselessly lyrical prose is in quest of all that is most profoundly true, or human, in her characters. And, again like much of the work of the stage 2 Modernist poets, many of whom turned from the "man-in-Brazil syndrome" toward a more religious or metaphysical preoccupation with "man-in-the-universe" themes,[9] Clarice Lispector's work sought what was most basic, communal, and universal in man.

Although she nearly always utilizes women protagonists as the crucibles in which these psychic quests for self-awareness and authenticity of being are continually tested, Lispector's primary concern is with the universal aspects of each person's "inner drama."[10] With the exception of *A hora da estrela,* all of Lispector's post-1961 work transcends the universal to touch, finally, on the cosmic and archetypal. This essentially mythopoetic, nonregionalistic approach to fiction writing is actually present in all of Lispector's work, including that written before *A maçã no escuro,*[11] but it becomes a dominant feature only after 1961. Standing, then, in stark contrast to the often heavy-handed sociopolitical fiction of the 1930s and 1940s, the subtle yet powerful *Perto do coração selvagem* amounted to an open challenge to the predictable, socially rooted literature that had been the norm in Brazil for so long. Praised by the noted critic Antônio Cândido at the time of its appearance as the first Brazilian novel to attempt a systematic conversion of language from instrument into subject matter,[12] *Perto do coração selvagem* heralded a new era for Brazilian fiction, one that had its immediate precursors, however, in the efforts of such writers as Cyro dos Anjos, Cornélio Pena, Otávio de Faria, and Lúcio Cardoso, the latter Lispector's friend, mentor, and confidant at the Agência Nacional.

During the late 1950s the Brazilian novel, like other forms of Western literature, began to be influenced by the French *nouveau roman*.[13] With its emphasis on the connection between language and three-dimensional reality, the novels of Alain Robbe-Grillet, Michel Butor, and Nathalie Sarraute made a significant impact on a generation of writers in Brazil. As the most outstanding member of this generation, Clarice Lispector's work has certain things in common with the French writers. Yet there is no solid evidence that Lispector consciously adopted either the themes or the techniques of the nouveau roman. Rather, as Gregory Rabassa has pointed out, her case seems to be one of a similar yet separate response to related issues and less a case of direct influence than one might think.[14] For unlike the French "new novelists," Lispector was less interested in "objectively" reporting the shape and appearance of "things" than in unraveling the skein of responses these "things" elicited in a perceiving mind. So although Lispector shares with Robbe-Grillet, Butor, and Sarraute a preoccupation with language and an enthusiasm for rejecting traditional plot structures, the Brazilian writer is more interested than the French writers in recording the various psychological states of her characters.[15] In this, Lispector shows herself to be closer to Sarraute than to Robbe-Grillet or Butor. Like Virginia Woolf, Djuna Barnes, and Albert Camus, Lispector is essentially concerned with showing the multiple, often conflicting responses of a human consciousness to specific external stimuli, such as an apple *(A maçã no escuro)* a cockroach *(A paixão segundo G. H.)*, or a blind man chewing gum ("Amor"). Thus, for Clarice Lispector, there is a distinct and constant phenomenological orientation to her work, which became more indirect and diffuse, however, as she matured as a writer. The phenomenological aspect of her work reached its zenith in *A paixão segundo G. H.* and then became less obvious, but no less important, in such later works as *O Lustre, Uma aprendizagem ou o livro dos prazeres, Água viva, A hora da estrela,* and *Um sopro de vida,* all of which concentrate more on lyrical explorations of self rather than on any dramatic discovery of relationships between self and world.

Reminiscent of Robbe-Grillet's *Les Gommes* (1953), Butor's *La Modification* (1957), and Sarraute's *Martereau* (1954), Lispector's fourth novel, *A maçã no escuro* is strongly keyed to the mercurial relationship between the protagonist's sense of who he is and his varying levels of awareness of the physical things—the novel's *choisisme*—that surround him. But even in this markedly phenomenological novel, Lispector's basic concern remains, as Monegal has shown, not psychologizing but language:[16] what is language; how, as humans, do we use (and misuse) it, and what is its real importance for us? Within the context of Brazilian literature, this pronounced linguistic, structural, and cognitive concern on the part of the author shows clearly how Lispector's work fits into a line of technically innovative yet socially aware literature that begins in the modern era with *Macunaíma* and runs up through much of the poetry and prose of the stage 3 Modernists. One thinks, for example, of João Cabral de Melo Neto's *Uma faca só lâmina (A Knife All Blade,* trans., K. S. Keys) or Rosa's *Grande sertão: veredas* (1956; *The Devil to Pay in the Backlands,* trans. Taylor and de Onís) as being in the same context as Lispector's work. Lispector's connection to the Brazilian Modernists, then is based on a general belief in the desirability of literary reform and a particular belief that language, even more than characterization, theme, or social relevancy, was the writer's greatest concern.

But if we think of Clarice Lispector as another link in the Modernist chain, we must also recognize that her work helped prove that Brazilian literature could exist on a par with European literature. Yet Lispector's narratives have with very few exceptions had little to do with re-creating the "authentic" aspects of Brazilian culture or national identity, something that was very important to the early Modernists. This general (though not, as we shall see, total) absence of nationalistic concerns was what most set her early work apart from the kind of fiction and poetry that was being written in Brazil during the 1930s and early 1940s. Only critics like Sérgio Milliet and Antônio Cândido, who saw the potential in Lispector's work for creating a new kind of literature in Brazil, felt comfortable in praising it. Thematically and especially linguistically, then, Lispector's fiction should be ranked alongside that of Guimarães Rosa as embodying, in the words of Oswald de Andrade, the "high-purposed esthetics"[17] of early Brazilian Modernism. It can be said, finally, that the best experimental narrative of the 1950s and 1960s in Brazil was practiced in different though complementary ways by Guimarães Rosa, Nélida Piñon, and Clarice Lispector: Rosa for his creative ability to tap the old roots of his language and for his ingenious neologisms, Piñon for the richness of her lexicon, and Lispector for her experiments with syntax and rhythm patterns.[18]

An additional problem connected to Lispector's reception by the Brazilian reading public of the 1940s has to do with what is one of the most unique features of her work, her highly original voice. Up to the time of *Perto do coração selvagem,* Brazilian literature, again with the exception of the great Machado de Assis, had not seen a novelist who was able to combine serious philosophical inquiry with linguistic and structural virtuosity in such an affective fashion. But the very uniqueness of Lispector's voice, which won her praise from some critics, also led many readers to reject her for being too "difficult"[19] and for writing a kind of fiction that was not immediately applicable to the Brazilian social experience. More than anything else, this kind of negative reaction to Lispector's work suggests the presence of a literary narrowness often associated with national literatures that lack a secure sense of history and identity. It is odd that, while early Modernists such as Mário and Oswald de Andrade understood this problem clearly and tried to rectify it, the impulse to continue doing so was largely forgotten or pushed aside in the wave of intensely regionalistic, politically charged prose fiction of the 1930s and 1940s. The exception here, and the writer of this era who most resembles Clarice Lispector, is undoubtedly Graciliano Ramos,[20] whose own work, like that of Clarice Lispector, is personal, introspective, and broodingly expressive of the inner realm. But while the Northeastern novel, including Ramos's was basically masculine and rural in content and social in its orientation, Lispector's fictive world, as early as 1944 and *Perto do coração selvagem,* was psychological, feminist, and urban in content and introspective in orientation. Lispector's creation of an entire canon of feminist, urban, and psychological narrative was a first not only for Brazilian letters but for Latin American and perhaps even for North American literature as well.

There is one notable exception to this tendency, however. The novel *A maçã no escuro* mentions Brazil specifically as the place the story seems to occur,[21] even though Lispector typically denationalizes her characters and settings. Martim, for example, is the male protagonist of the novel yet he is consistently referred to not as an individual but generically as *o homem* ("the man"). And although we learn that the story takes place in Brazil, the setting is systematically described as a desert, with the images of darkness, aridity, and silence playing crucial roles in the narrative's development. Silence and darkness, in fact, along with continual references to "the moment," are the most fundamental motifs in all of Lispector's fiction,[22] the ones that recur most consistently in her work. Unlike the preceding generation's settings, and characters, who, like Amado's Antônio Balduíno (of *Jubiabá*), can only be appreciated in a certain socio-political context of Brazil's Northeast, Lispector's people and places are not restricted either geographically or temporally; Martim *(A maçã no escuro)*, Ana ("Amor," *Laços de família*), Macabéa *(A hora da estrela)*, and the nameless, faceless voice of *Água viva* all exist as characters beyond the confines of Brazilian time and space. They are identifiably Brazilians, but only in certain ways; their primary validity as characters lies in their universality, their "humanness."

But when we review Lispector's fiction it is manifestly clear that her dominant focus is the psychological condition of urban women. The social dimension of her fictive world derives from the varied effects other beings, often though not always men, have on her female characters. The story "Family Ties" offers us a prime example of how Lispector typically treats her presentation of human relationships. These other beings, in their phenomonological condition as objects of someone else's perception, produce a flow of epiphany-like flashes in the mind of the protagonist, who, more often than not in Lispector's fiction, is a middle-class woman living in some kind of urban environment. Joana of *Perto do coração selvagem* and Ana of "Amor" are the prototypes of this kind of character and experience. In her role as a female writer who writes primarily "about women," and setting aside the fact that in their all-too-human fear, confusion, and pain Lispector's men and women are indistinguishable, Clarice Lispector fits nicely into a strong tradition of Brazilian "women's" literature that dates back at least to 1752 and the writing of what some have advanced as the first Brazilian novel.[23]

Clarice Lispector as a Woman Writer in Latin America

To paraphrase the title of Kate Chopin's landmark American novel, the "awakening" of women writers in Latin America is rapidly becoming one of the major literary events of the late twentieth century. It is, moreover, one that should command the close attention of all people interested in literature and in the ancient and vital connection between literature and society. Because of its scope and the freshness of its perspective, this development is sure to play an important role in the continuing development of Latin American literature. Women writers, in fact, may well represent the next "boom" in Spanish American and Brazilian letters. Representing a collective voice not as yet adequately heard from, the women writers of Latin America have given a tremendous injection of energy and vitality to the system of what is already one of the most active, daring, and imaginative bodies of literature in the Western tradition. Based on a firm conviction that literature can effectively serve the muses of both art and social justice, the emergence and recognition of women writers like Carlotta O'Neill, María Mendoza, Alicia Jurado, Luisa Valenzuela, Griselda Gambaro, Nélida Piñon, Maria Alice Barroso, Lygia Fagundes Telles, and Clarice Lispector in Latin America will continue the liberating technical and linguistic strides already taken by such male writers as Borges, Cortázar, Fuentes, García Márquez, Vargas Llosa, Donoso, Amado, Rosa, and, of course, Machado de Assis.

But in so doing, this new women's literature, one being written by but not necessarily for women, can also be expected to work to improve the general standard of living in Latin America and to demand recognition of equality under law and assurance of basic human rights in all areas of life. Thus the new women's literature of Spanish America and Brazil is sociologically and psychologically oriented at the same time that it seeks its own distinctive, original voice, its own standards of artistic excellence, and its own hitherto untested modes of expression.

With works like *Perto do coração selvagem, Laços de família, Água viva,* and *A hora de estrela* illustrating all aspects of this new literary trend, the fiction of Clarice Lispector has established itself as the standard to be met. Working on the cutting edge of a technical and thematic revolution in the area of the modern Latin American novel, Clarice Lispector was as devoted to the craft of fiction as she was to the highest, most unifying principles of feminism.[24] And unless we, the critics and the reading public, are willing to allow the much-abused term "feminism" to degenerate into a synonym for separatism, intolerance, or vindictiveness, we can feel confident that Clarice Lispector would have applauded the words of Argentina's

Griselda Gambaro, who, speaking of the relationship of feminist thought to a work of literature, has said that "as a rule, a work is considered to touch on the theme of feminism when its leading characters are women and are repressed or in rebellion, but as far as I am concerned, a work is feminist insofar as it attempts to explain the mechanics of cruelty, oppression, and violence through a story that is developed in a world in which men and women exist."[25]

The consolidating beauty and strength of this statement, rallying, as it does, men and women together under the banner of justice, equality, and solidarity, suggest what principle is at the heart of the feminist impulse in Latin American literature: that literature, aside from its purely aesthetic function as art, can and should serve a useful social purpose. If it is well done, as in the case of Clarice Lispector, literature can achieve this elusive goal by speaking of the larger, eternal truths about the human condition and by bringing men and women together, as allies and not enemies, united in a common struggle against all forms of tyranny and oppression, psychological as well as political. Epitomizing the burgeoning involvement of women in Latin American drama, narrative, and poetry, Clarice Lispector and her work stand at the core of this new and exciting event.

Clarice Lispector and the New Latin American Narrative

Having blossomed intellectually in the cosmopolitanism of Rio de Janeiro, Lispector published *Perto do coração selvagem* when she was nineteen. Given her age and inexperience at the time of its writing (she was actually seventeen when she first began to piece it together) this first novel is an extraordinary achievement. Far from being a flawless work of art, it nevertheless represents a real turning-point for Brazilian fiction in this century. As such, *Perto do coração selvagem* was the first of a series of works that by 1961 and *A maçã no escuro* had established Clarice Lispector as one of Brazil's most important mid-twentieth-century authors.

In drawing the Brazilian novel away from the sometimes crudely wrought regionalism of the 1930s and 1940s, and toward a new concern with form and style, Clarice Lispector gave Brazilian fiction a legitimacy and respectability it might not otherwise have received for a long time. There is no doubt, as Emir Rodríguez Monegal notes, that Guimarães Rosa represents to the *novo romance brasileiro* ("new Brazilian novel") essentially what Juan Rulfo represents to the *nueva novela hispanoamericana* ("new Spanish American novel").[26] But to hold this view does not invalidate the idea that as early as 1944, two years before the publication of Rosa's still partially regionalistic *Sagarana,* Lispector's *Perto do coração selvagem* had already begun to alter people's opinions about what Brazilian fiction could be like. After 1956 and the publication of *Grande sertão: veredas* (The Devil to Pay in the Backlands), Rosa's presence in Brazilian literature eclipses that of Lispector, who nonetheless continued to exert a significant and positive influence on Brazilian narrative. And while it is clear that Lispector's importance was never wholly over-shadowed by Rosa, it must be understood that the latter's influence has become much more widely felt and appreciated than Lispector's. But while Rosa's fictive world was basically rural, masculine, and exterior in nature, Lispector's was more urban, feminine, and interior, and this was a significant development. Through it all, Clarice Lispector was a writer's writer whose popularity would be largely restricted to those who liked intellectually demanding, avantgarde fiction, and if she was never a popular author, she was always an important one. In summary, one is tempted to say that if Rosa was Brazil's James Joyce, then Clarice Lispector was its Virginia Woolf.

But if Lispector's *Perto do coração selvagem* appeared in print two years before Rosa's *Sagarana,* it also antedated by two years the publication of Miguel Angel Asturias's *El señor Presidente.* This latter novel, often cited as one of the major precursors of the "new novel" in Spanish America, was demonstrably different, in terms of its language, structure, and thematics, from the novels that preceded it. Yet Lispector's work, appearing two years earlier, is more uniformly and systematically innovative than the uneven and irregular Asturias work. Read from beginning to end *Perto do coração selvagem* makes it clear that its author was operating with not only a new vision of reality, one based on a philosophical, feminist (in that sense, "political"), and phenomenological conception of existence, but with some radically new ideas about how to express this vision literarily. This attempt to reconcile the inner and outer realms of human existence finds an especially poignant expression in the semiotically fascinating second novel, *O lustre,* and in such stories as "Daydreams of a Drunk Woman," "The Dinner," and "Temptation."

One of the most important of these "new ideas," Lispector's experimentations with language as human sign system, came to be connected integrally to her thematic concerns about human consciousness, identity, and the process of characterizational self-realization. It has been said in this regard that Clarice Lispector's work "reveals an almost maniacal determination to use the right word, to exhaust the possibilities of each word, to build up a solid structure of words."[27] Like her renowned countryman João Guimarães Rosa, Lispector placed a special significance on the role language would play in her narratives. In Lispector's fiction, language is not only an issue of style; it is, recalling the work of critics like Barthes and Genette, both a subject of hermeneutic inquiry itself and the all too flawed method by which that very hermeneutic inquiry is undertaken. As with Rosa's *Grande sertão: veredas,* Borges's *Ficciones,* Cabrera Infante's *Tres tristes tigres* (Three trapped tigers), and Sarduy's *Cobra,* language, in its seemingly endless capacity to reflect on itself and on the ever-changing relationships it can establish among beings in the world, emerges as the signal feature in nearly all Lispector's fiction. It is essentially on this issue of the importance of language to narrative—to its structuring and to its semiotic signification or "meaning"—that Lispector shows her link to the "new novelists" of Spanish America.

Brazil, oddly, has not yet enjoyed the same kind of international recognition that the so-called "Boom" in Spanish American literature has achieved. But, as Gregory Rabassa once observed,[28] Brazil may actually possess greater unity and continuity in the development of its national literature because of the numbers of skilled writers it has produced in the various genres and because of its historical stability. Nevertheless, it is only very recently, as José Donoso has written in his *A Personal History of the "Boom,"*[29] that the nations of Spanish America have begun to emerge from their cultural isolation, or "solitude," and read the books being written in other Latin American countries. And although Brazil is still a large unknown entity to many people, writers as well as scholars, it has made considerable progress, especially in the second half of the twentieth century, toward recognition and appreciation by its hemispheric neighbors. Within this process of international cross-fertilization, the work of Clarice Lispector takes on a particular importance; in fact, judging from the innovative style, structure, and themes of her first novel, she can be said to have perhaps written the first "new novel" in Latin America.

In later works, such as *A paixão segundo G. H.* and *Água viva*, Lispector proved that she was making a career out of writing the kind of fiction that, in Spanish America, was being touted as a new mode of novel writing, one replete with new themes (or new treatments of old ones), new styles, and new techniques. Teresinha Alves Pereira has shown, for example, the technical coincidences that exist between Lispector's *A maçã no escuro* and Julio Cortázar's *Rayuela*.[30] Other parallels can be shown to exist between Lispector's work and the efforts of such Spanish American narrativists as Guillermo Cabrera Infante, Severo Sarduy, José Donoso, Juan Carlos Onetti, Carlos Fuentes, Gabriel García Márquez, and José Lezama Lima.[31] The power of Lispector's fiction, her unmistakable style, her "open" structures, and her variations on a single thematic line (the depiction of human consciousness) all tend to solidify her position as a leader in the post–World War II vanguard of revisionist novelists and short-story writers in Brazil[32] and Spanish America, a vanguard that parallels the rise of Postmodernism in Western literature.

But beyond the attention paid to language, the "new" Latin American novel, whether written by Clarice Lispector or one of her Spanish American counterparts, is also characterized by its acute sensitivity to structure. Indeed, as David Gallagher has observed, in reading these "new" novels one gets the distinct impression that their form derives directly from the kind of things their authors are writing about.[33] And because this means that, in the "new" Latin American novel, form is indivisible from content, from "meaning," it is clear how modern Latin American narrative, much of which is distinctively Postmodernist in character, has given new importance to the role phenomenology plays in the organization and presentation of the story. Latin American literature, moreover, has developed this way largely on its own and not because of servile imitations of foreign models, which have, of course, been known to the "new" Latin American writers, the French *nouveau roman* being a case in point. But these foreign models have, since World War II, been regarded more as possibilities rather than patterns that had to be followed in order to write "good" literature. Indeed, the case of Borges suggests that the situation may have been just the opposite.

And just as Clarice Lispector was an early experimenter in terms
of the roles language could take in fictional creativity, so too was
she in the vanguard of those Latin American writers who, because
of the challenges presented by their new themes, felt constrained
to impose new kinds of form on their narratives. This reflects the
basic theoretical justification for what came to be called *realismo
mágico* (literally, "magical realism"), a way of presenting a story that
very naturally blends the fantastic with the ordinary, the logical
with the impossible. One has only to think of *Um sopro de vida,
Perto do coração selvagem,* or "Miss Ruth Algrave" to see how this
new concept about how a writer might structure his or her work
applies to what Clarice Lispector set out to do. And while if read
hermeneutically each of her narratives deals to some degree with a
personal revelation, each of them also possesses an inner unity that
is its own, a unity that does not stem from some externally imposed
notion about "how a novel should be structured," but from the
nature of the material involved in the story. The odyssey-like and
circular structure of *A maçã no escuro,* for example, parallels the
linguistic quest undertaken by the protagonist, Martim. The poetrylike, confessional form of much of *Água viva* and especially of
Um sopro de vida comes not from an interest to write polyphonic
prose but from the narrative voice's struggle to understand and
express what was happening to her, to capture in words the essence
of her deeply private experience. And in *A hora da estrela,* the
extrinsic sociological implications spring naturally from the self-
conscious and fallible narrator's musings about herself, about the
nature of the relationship between human creativity and art and
between art and society, specifically Brazil's Northeast.

It is perhaps ironic that it is *A hora da estrela,* Lispector's penultimate novel, that most forcefully and unambiguously demonstrates
a third characteristic of the modern Latin American novel: its realization that language, inextricably bound up in the problems of
semiotics and phenomenology, cannot ever be trusted to do what
we want it to do (which involves a question of technique) or be
what we want it to be (which touches on the issue of theme). As a
human invention utilized by humans, language is perfect only as
an ideal; in human hands, it becomes a highly imperfect expression
of our uncertainties, mistakes, ignorance, creativity and curiosity,
our hopes, anxieties, fears, and desires. In short, language is the
only tool we have that is both subject and object, simultaneously

the thing studied and the manner of study. Modern Latin American novels are often prolix not because their authors simply wish to write long, difficult books; they are so because in recognizing, as Martim, G. H., and the voice of *Água viva* do, both the beauty and the ultimate treachery of words, they choose to combat the cultural, political, psychological, and linguistic problems that envelop man in his struggle to know and to communicate this knowledge to others. Among the many Latin American narrativists of the late twentieth century, Lispector figures among the most adept at showing how the eternal human struggle with words, with communication, tragically culminates all too often in a state of silence. Her intense tales make one wonder whether meaningful human communication is ever really possible. Only the laconic voices of *Pedro Páramo* rival Lispector's in their ability to effect an atmosphere of barren silence, to cloak themselves in a kind of total solitude that even language, that most miraculous of gifts, cannot break. But, as Benedito Nunes shows in *O mundo de Clarice Lispector*, what Lispector does to and with language in her work is simply the response of one artist to the greater question of how language plays a role in the writing, structuring, and decoding of a story or novel. Other Latin American novels of this ilk include Mario Vargas Llosa's *Conversación en La Catedral* (1970; Conversation in the Cathedral). Cabrera Infante's *Tres tristes tigres*, Rosa's *Grande sertão: veredas*, Sarduy's *Cobra* (1972), Donoso's *El obsceno pájaro de la noche* (1973; The obscene bird of night), and García Márquez's *El otoño del patriarca* (1975; *The Autumn of the Patriarch*), but the list runs easily much longer. Yet when we examine both her themes and the various techniques by which she gives form to these themes, it becomes clear that Clarice Lispector stands "close to the savage heart" of the entire "new novel" movement in Latin America. Although not yet properly acknowledged in this regard[34] Clarice Lispector was both a forerunner of the "new novel" in Latin America and, by 1977, one of its ablest practitioners as well.

Phenomenology and the "New Novel" of Clarice Lispector

Virtually all of Clarice Lispector's fiction shows itself to be deeply involved with the psychological processes peculiar to phenomenology. Directly or indirectly, Lispector wrote nearly always about the tensions and ecstasies bound up in the development of a private consciousness, a consciousness that was nevertheless afflicted with the sense of dread, isolation, and "nausea"[35] that we associate with Existentialism. As a "new novelist," Clarice Lispector merged the narrative strength of the traditional realistic novel and its ability to tell a story with the suggestive music, power, nuance, and ambiguity of lyric poetry. The result was truly a new kind of novel, one that told a story not about concretely described characters in action within a three-dimensional world but relied on symbol, metaphor, and verbal patterning to delve into the nature and act of consciousness itself. Never forgetting that there simultaneously exist innumerable levels, degrees, and kinds of interaction between our public and private existences, Lispector leads her protagonists to verbalize, or attempt to verbalize, those acts of cognition in which their awarenesses, coming into often unexpected contact with other objects, react to them in a fluid, associational fashion. G. H., of *A paixão segundo G. H.,* undergoes this kind of basically mystical experience after she crushes the cockroach:

What had I done? . . . I had killed. I had killed! But why that exultation and, more than that, why the deep-rooted acceptance of the exultation? How long, then, had I been capable of killing? No, that was not the question. The question was rather: what had I killed?

The serene woman I had always been, had she gone mad with pleasure? With my eyes still closed I was quaking with exultation. To have killed: it was so much greater than I, it was as high as the boundless room that contained me. To have killed opened up the aridity of the sands of the room to the damp, at last, at last, as if I had dug and dug with hard and eager fingers until I discovered within myself the drinkable thread of life which, in reality, was the thread of death. I slowly opened my eyes, gently now, in gratitude and diffidence, ashamed at my splendor.

Free of the damp world from which I had at last emerged, I opened my eyes and saw again the great, harsh, bare light; I saw the door of the wardrobe, now closed. And I saw half of the cockroach's body protruding from the door.[36]

In a similar case, that pertaining to Martim, the Everyman protagonist of *A maçã no escuro,* the reader accompanies Martim on a psychic odyssey, or quest (though an ironic one, to be sure), that carries him from a state of self-induced unconsciousness to one of consciousness, or awareness. Like G. H., Martim also performs an act of self-liberating violence; G. H. crushes the cockroach while Martim believes he has killed his wife. Once "freed" by his act, Martim's inner journey toward higher awareness is traced metaphorically as he encounters things (objects) of a progressively more advanced order in the biological chain of being; he moves (physically and psychologically) from rocks to vermin to birds and then to larger animals until he finally enters the realm of human beings once again.[37] A critical phenomenological moment in *A maçã no escuro,* and a scene that is reminiscent of Roquentine's famous encounter with the chestnut tree in Sartre's *La Nausée* (1938), involves Martim's experience with the cows:

His contact with the cows was a painful effort. . . . With an intelligence brought on by the very inferiority of his situation, he let himself remain submissive and attentive. Then, sacrificing his own identification, he almost took on the form of one of the animals. . . . He himself did not understand . . . but was growing little by little. . . . But it was also true that in that moment joie de vivre had already come over him. . . . With trembling joy he felt that something had happened. . . .[38]

From a reading of these two examples, we can get an accurate idea of how Lispector structures her fiction by focusing on the shifting relationships between things in the universe and our apprehension of them. By building her narratives around this kind of phenomenological relationship, Lispector calls the reader's attention to the crucial role language plays in our sense of reality and identity, of who and what we are. This acute concern over language (and how it is used), reality, and our ability to deal with both is one of the chief distinguishing features of the "new" Latin American novel and is one of Clarice Lispector's most distinctive features as a novelist. Relentlessly probing this ephemeral, allusive linkage between language and its ability both to create and to control reality (including, as in *A hora da estrela* and *Um sopro de vida,* the very text we are reading), Lispector forces her characters to confront the truth about themselves and their place in the universe. Occasionally, as with Joana, G. H., Lóri, and the voice of *Água viva,* this confrontation is positive and can be expected to lead to a more satisfying and authentic existence. But more often, as in the case of Virgínia, Martim, Ana, Macabéa, or Mrs. Jorge B. Xavier, the confrontation of self and universe is too terrifying to withstand, too destructive of one's social and psychological status quo, and devastation results.

We observe in the cases of G. H. and Martim, however, how "intentionality," the pivotal concept in Husserl's theory of phenomenology, enables both characters to distill or bracket their experiences, thereby allowing them to enter, perhaps imperfectly, into the totality of a new, higher level of awareness and being. In the fiction of Clarice Lispector, the ultimate intent or effect of this constant phenomenological tension between a consciousness and the world of objects it perceives is to allow her protagonists to get beyond themselves, to escape, momentarily (as in the cases of Martim and Ana) or more permanently (as with G. H.), from the psychological prisons in which their conventionally used language and their "inauthentic" social existences place them. The points at which these psychic "escapes" take place inevitably mark the most compelling moments of the story, the moments at which the lyrical expressiveness is at its height. Although the stories of Ana, Martim, and G. H. illustrate three of the most succinct expressions of what Colin Wilson has called the "phenomenological shock"[39] in all of Lispector's work, it is a quality that is endemic to virtually all her fiction.

Because she is so intent upon entering into and reproducing the sundry psychic ramifications that derive from the process of human cognition and perception, Lispector was, from the beginning, obliged to create a linguistic medium that would be appropriate for her characters yet capable of accurately re-creating the essentially mystical experience that is her underlying concern. The language that she employs in her fiction, therefore, is both demotic and incantatory,[40] superficially facile yet hypnotic in its emotive suggestiveness. So compelling is Lispector's concern with language, consciousness, and reality that many of her works demand recognition as numbering among the finest Postmodernist "language novels" yet produced in Latin America.

Noting her acute sensitivity to language and human consciousness, one of Lispector's most perceptive critics has noted that, because of her "mythological turn of mind,"[41] she is actually a sorceress with words, striving always to harness the hidden power of her lexicon to play upon the reader's imagination, intellect, and emotions. Rather than rely on the plot structurings and descriptions of the realistic novel, Lispector makes use of patterns of imagery, recurring scenes and symbols, repetition, and rhythmic sentences to establish a distinctly poetic view of the world and its innumerable levels of reality and meaning. This explains why the language Lispector uses in her stories, and especially in her later novels (e.g., *A maçã no escuro, Água viva* and *Um sopro de vida*), regularly has more in common with poetry, and especially modern poetry, than with the methods of realistic narrative. Hers is a rhythmical, metonymic, and oxymoronic prose, rich in similes, paradox, and imagery and suggesting always the active, fecund presence of yet another reality, one composed of myth, ritual, and ultimate beginnings.

In Lispector's fictive world, therefore, objects (e.g., cows, cockroaches, blind men chewing gum) prompt the protagonist to question the nature and meaning of human existence in new and startling ways. These objects point, counterpoint, and draw the characters who behold them into a self-reflectiveness that deepens their understanding of self, world, and interhuman relationships. But at the same time, these same concretely depicted objects also underscore the tragic and inescapable fact that human beings and their world can never be conjoined. Ultimately, in Lispector's fiction (with the possible exception of *Um sopro de vida* or *Uma aprendizagem ou o livro dos prazeres,* in which love alone succeeds in bridging the essential isolation of people), the existential anguish and sense of absurdity that result from one's becoming aware—as Lispector's characters do—of the temporality and isolation of the human condition win out. Although like Catarina of the story "Laços de família" *(Family Ties),* Joana of *Perto do coração selvagem,* or G. H., Lispector's characters often attain a state of authentic freedom for themselves, they also realize that they will have to live out their lives alone, that freedom, while it can be given, cannot be shared. Like Sartre, Lispector understood that we are indeed "condemned to being free."

As an artist, Clarice Lispector was essentially concerned with reproducing the ebb and flow of human consciousness, with tracing its uncertain relationship with other beings, and with transforming it into the structural framework of her narratives. The trivial, external events of which she writes (like G. H.'s crushing of the roach) function as catalysts, touching off the protagonist's relentless, self-seeking search for an awareness and wholeness that transcend three-dimensional reality, the temporal and spatial limitations imposed by the mimetically rendered reality, and the objective norms of the realistic novel. This tendency, too, is an aspect of the "new" Latin American novel that Clarice Lispector shares with her Spanish American counterparts. But Lispector, utilizing phenomenology as both method of inquiry and subject matter, existentialism as her ethical base, and a highly lyrical prose as her medium of expression, succeeds in bridging the gap between the inner and outer realms, between reality and our contemplation of it. In so doing, her work represents one of the most complete expressions of this philosophical-cum-poetic vision of the human experience that we as yet have had in the world of Latin American letters.

Chapter Three
Some Intrinsic Considerations: Style, Structure, and Point of View

Evident as early as *Perto do coração selvagem,* Lispector's basic mode of expression was lyrical in both style and structure. Her novels and short stories, while intensely poetic, are not "psychological" narratives, not, at least, insofar as this elusive term is defined as relating principally to fiction that depicts mental processes or developments, such as neurosis. Even in a story like "The Imitation of the Rose," in which a woman is seen recovering from an unspecified mental disorder, the primary focus is not on the nature or effect of the malady itself but on the way a particular human mind, "well" or not, receives stimuli from the physical world, synthesizes these, and refashions them into patterns of reference that are meaningful to the protagonist, the person whose perspective dominates the narrative and determines the story's structure.

Lispector's fiction characteristically reflects a constant concern for an appreciation and presentation of the protagonists's complex, mysterious, and often contradictory personality, the sentient and ceaselessly self-reflective mind. This concern, plus the effort made to relate the mind to the world of "others" that surrounds it, gives her lyrically structured narratives a decidedly phenomenological inclination. As is manifestly evident in several stories from *Laços de família* and in such novels as *A cidade sitiada, A maçã no escuro,* and *Uma aprendizagem, ou o livro dos prazeres,* the crucial process of depicting an expanding consciousness assumes both an internal and an external form, one that, virtually without exception in Lispector's fiction, connects the way we perceive the outer world (our cognition of it) and the various ways we comprehend it (our utilization of it, the ways we make it meaningful to us). Benedito Nunes, Lispector's most complete critic, casts new light on this crucial issue in his excellent *Leitura de Clarice Lispector.* In so doing, he shows how

several of the theories of Poststructuralism can be illuminatingly
applied to Lispector's narratives.

Style

Because the process by which Clarice Lispector establishes her
highly unique fictive world, one dominated by an acutely self-aware
protagonist awash psychologically in a world of disconnected objects
and perceptions, rests on the issue of style, the reader cannot fully
understand what Lispector is writing about until he or she takes a
close look at how she writes. It has been said that "no one writes
like she does,"[1] a comment that justly calls attention to the fact
that Clarice Lispector was a writer possessed of an unusually original
and identifiable style. As with Machado de Assis and Guimarães
Rosa, to whom she can be revealingly compared as regards the
uniqueness of her style, Clarice Lispector was very conscious of how
she wrote.[2] Although more research needs to be done concerning
the exact nature of the creative and highly original process by which
she transformed her randomly taken notes into finished manuscripts,
which invariably demonstrate an unmistakable style and structuring,
we can say Lispector's style was organically connected to her subject
matter, the phenomenological issues of cognition, signification, and
self-realization that dominated her work.

Approaching her fiction from a stylistic perspective, we find that
the syntactical features of her novels and short stories constitute her
most singular stylistic characteristic. More than the way words are
arranged in a sentence, syntax, for a sophisticated fiction writer,
refers immediately to the way, given the grammatical structures of
a particular language system, a person apprehends the universe. But
beyond merely determining how we "see" the world, how we "understand" it, syntax, through the grammatical "laws" that govern
its usage, actually determines what the world becomes for us, what
we think it "is." Syntax, then, determines not only how we view
life, but what it consists of as well. Hence, for a writer like Clarice
Lispector, whose most constant concern is over both what reality is
like and how each of us deals with its manifold aspects and its
mutability, syntax resides at the heart of any serious discussions of
her style. Lispector's syntactical deformation of the traditional Portuguese sentence is done, consciously or not, to force us to define
and interpret the world differently, to require, by connecting words

in new and frequently startling ways (and by using "old" words in "new" ways), that the reader hermeneutically accompany the author on a voyage of discovery into the uncharted reaches of reality and possible apprehensions of it.[3]

The typical Lispectorian sentence varied dramatically during the author's career. In her early work, especially that which preceded *A maçã no escuro,* Lispector's sentences were predominantly "nonperiodic," or conversational in their structure, although one could also find many sentences that were more "periodic" in essence. Normally we associate the periodic sentence with rather formal writing, but in the case of Clarice Lispector we note that while the effect of the periodic sentence is retained, its traditional length and oratorical quality are not. Lispector's sentences have always tended to be short, even cryptic in length, but, like the periodic sentence, their message remains open to interpretation, the uncertainty extending beyond the grammatical closure normally provided by the syntax. Examples of this kind of sentence abound in Lispector's work, even in her pre-1961 novels, which may fairly be considered as being less uniformly lyrical in design than most of the later material. The stories show a different development, however.

Additional characteristics of her sentences have to do with parataxis, that is, a writing style that strings together the members of a sentence without a clear explanation of their connection, and hypotaxis, a style in which the members of a sentence are clearly connected by conjunctions, clauses, and subordinate clauses. The paratactic style of a Hemingway or a Guimarães Rosa is also present in the work of Clarice Lispector; like that of the American writer, Lispector's prose is simple and spare, even stark in its expressiveness (though not in its lyrical patterning), and like her countryman's, Lispector's fiction is full of words (that is, symbolically expressed ideas) put one after another that do not at first glance appear to be at all related. The style of Rosa and the style of Lispector at first appear to be quite different, yet closer observation proves their respective styles to have more in common than one would think; both styles are highly self-conscious in terms of their linguistic function, both are innovative, and both are highly recognizable. A primary difference, however, is that Rosa's onomatopoeias, neologisms, and portmanteau words make his style more obviously inventive while Lispector's more subtle syntactical deformations are less easily discerned. The style of each writer, however, places great demands on the reader. As though she were consciously writing poetry and not narrative, Clarice Lispector, always lyrical in her efforts to break the imprisoning chains of standard syntax, employed both hypotactic and paratactic sentences. In so doing, she keeps the reader "off balance" and puts him into contact with ideas, associations, or fragments of the cognitive process that free him from the restraints of syntactic orthodoxy. This requires him to apprehend reality the way it "really" is (paradoxical, ambiguous and uncertain), as opposed to the way we are conditioned to see it (as a knowable, manageable entity) through the inauthentic forms that constitute our worn-out, stereotypical language use.

The famous ambiguity of Lispector's fiction is, in its rendering, as much a thematic feature as a stylistic one, in particular a syntactic one. In "Family Ties," which is one of Lispector's most fully realized artistic achievements, this sense of ambiguity arises not out of a desire for duplicity on the characters' part but out of a "realistic" confusion over what is going on (the reality, or more properly, "realities") around them and an even greater confusion over how they can deal with it, how they can control life by assigning words to it. Consistent with Lispector's view that each of us fights this battle for control of the chaos that envelops us, she shows poignantly how the woman in the story is growing in terms of consciousness and self-understanding—tangled as this itself is— while the man with whom she is living (and with whom, presumably, she has had, in social terms a "close" or "intimate" relationship) is stupidly and dully trapped in his own uninteresting view of reality, a view that, as a close reading of his comments shows, is entirely dominated by the spurious "clarity" of his conventional thought, his socially prescribed clichés and unoriginal "thinking."

In *Tractatus Logico-Philosophicus* Wittgenstein argues that we should remain silent about that which we cannot formulate into words. On the basis of her style, Clarice Lispector seems to believe just the contrary, that as conscious, sensitive human beings we cannot resist attempting to articulate that which, because of the failure of language, we are incapable of formulating in words. Hence, the basic paradox of all Lispector's work: our language compels us to do what we cannot do—use language to explain what we do when we use language. It is within this shadowy realm of uncertain and hidden meaning, of off-center ambiguity within the territory of imprecise, vague, unnamed objects and impulses, that Lispector chooses to operate. As she believes, it is the fluttering, anguished movement between "knowing" and "not knowing" that reflects the unique manner in which each creature, if only for an instant, feels about being alive. Such a vague, amorphous subject is necessarily involved with speaking about that which we cannot truly speak, an aspect of Lispector's work that underscores the pervasive spirit of noncommunication running through her fiction. Her hermetic, ambiguous style, then, amounts to a kind of concrete manifestation of her basic thematic concerns.

Lispector's novels have never, even from the first, been what one might describe as "noisy" or full of sound. Silence, a characteristic of much Postmodernist literature,[4] has always been a unique hallmark of her prose, one that has grown steadily in terms of its presence in her work. In *Água viva,* the silence of inner rumination achieves a kind of apotheosis, becoming an all-consuming force itself, one that for the protagonist as well as for the reader becomes entrancing and anesthetizing. The anxious, intensely self-inquisitorial tone of her fiction recalls Sartre's *La Nausée* (1938) and Camus's *Le Mythe de Sisyphe* (1942). These three authors, Lispector, Camus, and Sartre, blend literature and philosophy into something new and unique, a kind of narrative in which the style or medium is indeed the message. This is especially true in terms of Lispector and Camus, the two authors of this triad most concerned, paradoxically, with using language to show us how language fails to communicate effectively for us.

Stylistically, lyrical fiction represents a special instance of the novel of awareness. In the case of Clarice Lispector, the distinctive qualities of her lyrical fiction must be found in the narrative modes[5] by which her characters apprehend reality (and their own consciousness), as well as in the way images are formed and employed in the verbal presentation of the apprehension. This, the process of portraiture, constitutes one of the chief distinguishing differences between lyrical and nonlyrical fiction.[6] In *A maçã no escuro,* for example, or *A paixão segundo G. H.,* the portrait of the respective protagonists is drawn in what seems to be a timeless vacuum, a universe that has lost its sense of time and space for the apprehending humans who inhabit it. Again, it is this pervasive sense of timelessness that conjures up within the deep, dark recesses of the mind of Martim, Virgínia, Lóri, Lucrécia, Joana, and G. H., minds that remind us of Jung's "collective unconscious," stirrings of ties to a primordial, unconscious existence. In this fashion, Lispector's version of the lyrical novel continues to project a distinctive, unique quality and promises to increase the author's stature in the world of Latin American literature.

The development of Clarice Lispector as a writer of lyrical fiction, which was hinted at structurally and stylistically as early as in her first three novels, is similar to that of James Joyce, whose literary growth can be traced from *Dubliners* (1916) through *Finnegans Wake* (1939). Lispector's literary evolution has been rather unique in Latin American letters in that it has been remarkably consistent, steady, and clear. In each successive work from 1944 through 1977, Lispector has wrought an even greater dominance of the inner, subjective world (silence) over the outer, objective world (sound). As early as 1944 Álvaro Lins had noted that the style of Lispector's prose was strongly "poetic" and many critics discussed both its marked, though irregular, cadence and its extensive usage of figurative language and imagery.[7] To take an example of prose poetry, the style of *Perto do coração selvagem* is predominantly prosaic, (that is, it has a definite narrative line), but it borrows from the enriching characteristics of pure poetry, especially in its rhythm, diction, and imagery.

Defining style as how Lispector says what she wishes to say, we should not neglect to note some of the other salient aspects, such as diction, of her very recognizable style. Lispector's language is characteristically that of ordinary speech; it is demotic, in the sense that Frye used the term,[8] reflecting not the rhythms of everyday Brazilian usage (for her syntactical arrangements are unique) but the vocabulary of educated but nonformal Brazilian speech. Lispector typically chooses nouns, both "concrete" and "abstract," that are easily recognized by most literate people. The titles of her novels and stories bear out this tendency: *Perto do coração selvagem, O lustre, A cidade sitiada, A maçã no escuro, A hora da estrela, Um sopro de vida,* "No fundo de gaveta," and "Amor." As is obvious from this partial list of titles, Lispector has a propensity for focusing our attention on a "simple" object, sentiment, or concept alluded to in the title; we are subtly led into new and surprising considerations of words that we thought we "knew." There is little about Lispector's diction that is troublesome for the reader. She is not, for example, so linguistically inventive as was her great countryman Guimarães Rosa nor is her vocabulary as lexically rich and varied as Nélida Piñon's.[9]

What is difficult about Lispector's diction is its deceptive simplicity; like much of the best modern poetry, her fiction is superficially simple and easy to read but, upon closer reflection, difficult to interpret. Interested as she always was in the ever uncertain and shifting relationships between words and the various realities they purport to stand for, Lispector wrote fiction that constantly challenges the reader to do what she herself did, to mull ceaselessly over words and concepts until every last bit of denotation and connotation had been extracted from them. But as Lispector also knew well (indeed as every writer must know), in the final analysis there is no "end" to what any word can "mean." This is so because of language's most crucial yet most mysterious quality—the fact that at any given moment its "meaning" is dependent not only on conventional acceptance but, more importantly, on the ability of our imagination, our creativity, to imbue it with new meanings and new associations. For someone interested in "reader response" criticism, Lispector's work offers a wealth of fascinating material. The "simple" diction of Clarice Lispector is like a steel spring that has been compressed and then tied. The reader, who by the act of reading (with all the cognitive effort the term implies) "unties" the spring, senses that he is struck by a multitude of unexpected meanings for words he thought he "knew" thoroughly. The polysemy of language is, as for poets, an issue much at the heart not only of how Lispector writes but of what she writes about. Guimarães Rosa is said to have remarked of Lispector's work that he always learned new meanings for "old" words, but that he, personally, did not care for her overall style, her method of delivery.[10]

On the surface, Lispector's style seems like fine white porcelain, brilliant, hard, and unyielding yet translucent and mysteriously entrancing. In its own way it challenges the reader to "understand" reality (or "realities") in much the same way as Rosa does in his fiction, especially *Grande sertão: veredas*. Although the style of these two writers, both giants in the evolution of twentieth-century Latin American narrative, is markedly different in nearly all ways, their styles are similar in that, in each case, they reflect a deep and abiding concern over language as being the most crucial factor in novel writing. It is in this sense that we see how Clarice Lispector and Guimarães Rosa revolutionized Brazilian narrative in the second half of the twentieth century.

Another aspect of Lispector's style that deserves close attention is her use of figurative language. In her constant struggle to break out of the intellectual stagnation caused by living a life that is built on both the deadening pressure of materialism and the state of nonthinking conformity that attends it (a struggle that the reader experiences through the characters), Lispector relies heavily on tropes, linguistic usages that in their context are different from the "standard" meanings (the programmed nonthinking of most social discourse) of "literal" (nonimaginative, or denotative) language. The point is that Lispector's implementation of figurative language shows her protagonists experiencing epiphanylike moments of awareness. They come to grips with themselves, with who and what they really are and, finally, react to this unexpectedly experienced flash of insight by either rejecting the "new self" that would emerge or by actually undertaking the creation of a new self, a new and authentic identity. Lispector's sense, then, of the function of figurative language in her fiction is to draw her characters, as well as herself and the reader, closer to the core, closer to the essence of a personal sense of being, of identity. Paralleling what happens in the "real world," Lispector's characters are shown in the process of establishing a sense of personal identity (whether or not they are willing to lie to themselves about who they are, and why, is a closely related issue) by speculating endlessly on what has "happened," what it "means" to them and how they will "respond" to it. But the price of real freedom is always high and appears in Lispector's fiction as the discomfiting and solipsistic realization that we are all alone, isolated in our solitude, and tormented by the need to communicate. But in our anguish, we are "close," as Lispector and Joyce knew, "to the savage heart of life," close to the truth, often unpleasant and frightening, about who and what we are, and this is Lispector's real subject matter.

Closely allied with Lispector's manipulation of tropes, which are more germane to meaning than to rhetorical form, are the figures of speech she employs. As generally understood, figures of speech do not involve extensions of outright changes of denotative meaning, as do the more radical tropes, but rather a variation of form and pattern, both of which are, as we have seen, central to Freedman's definition of the lyrical novel. Certain "rhetorical figures," such as those involving darkness, silence, water, and language, are employed systematically by Lispector to create particular scenes and moments, scenes and moments that inevitably focus on the ebb and flow of the protagonist's consciousness. Some of these figures, such as simile and metaphor, are an easily discernible part of Lispector's style, while others, like the use of metonymy, synecdoche, personification, paradox, and oxymoron, are more subtle in their function.

Of the first group, Lispector relies heavily on similes and metaphors to transfer one kind of quality, or meaning, to another. This aspect of her style, poetic in nature, allows her to involve her characters in ontological ruminations about themselves and their place in the world. Thus we see once again how Lispector's basic style directly affects the subjects about which she writes, and vice versa. Her metaphors, implicit and mixed, all serve to assist the author in her creation of a fictional world characterized by a rich and powerful inner speculation that is imprisoned in its existentially perceived isolation. A signal feature of Lispector's style in this regard is that the medium of expression—language—is immediately entered into and responded to by the attentive reader who, along with the character, slowly comes to realize that while language can make us aware of our solitude it cannot free us from that solitude. This is the basic dilemma for Lispector's characters, from Joana to the poetic "I" of *Um sopro de vida,* and, thanks to her imagistic, rhythmic style, it is acutely sensed by the reader, who participates in the telling or expressing of a story as if he were reading a lyric poem.

Closely related to the presence of figurative language in Lispector's prose style is her ability to create patterns of rhythm in her tales. In addition to being syntactically innovative, basically simple in terms of its diction, and highly figurative in terms of its language use, Lispector's prose has the balanced, controlled movement of good poetry. Although one can see her tropes, similes, and metaphors, for example, by reading her prose silently, one must read it aloud to hear its inner rhythms and euphony. To appreciate better its musicality, we can turn to almost any page of Lispector's writings, *Um sopro de vida,* for example, and begin to read aloud. Though not as pronounced as with pure lyric poetry, the surge of her prose makes itself felt. One can look to a work such as *Água viva,* the most thoroughly poetic of all her works, and find pages that are rhythmic not only in terms of diction but in form and structure on the page as well:

It's hard for me to believe that I will die . . . because I'm bubbling
with cool freshness . . . my life will be very long because each instant
is. I have the impression that I'm about to be born and I cannot achieve
it.
   I'm a heart beating in the world.
   You who read me, help me to be born.
   Wait . . . it's getting dark.
   Darker . . . and darker.
   The instant is in total darkness.
   It continues.
   Wait . . . I'm beginning to glimpse something . . . a luminescent
form.   A milky belly with a navel? Wait . . . I will exit from this
darkness, where I am afraid. Darkness and ecstasy . . . I am the heart
of darkness.
   The problem is that the window of my room has a broken curtain rod,
and so the curtain doesn't close. Then the full moon comes in and the
room becomes phosphorescent with silence . . . it's horrible.
   Now the shadows are dissolving.
   I was born.
   Pause.
   Marvelous scandal . . . I'm being born.[11]

Typical of the style and structuring of Lispector's later fiction,
passages such as the one just cited speak to the reader more as lyric
poetry than as prose, even allowing for the loss, through the translation, of the original text's melody. This fact reinforces our basic
contention that, in its waxing and waning, its constant sense of
flow, of quest, Lispector's style simultaneously reflects and expresses
the ephemeral psychic state or nuance being experienced, if only for
an instant, by her protagonist. With the balance here shifting decidedly to intensely poetic, as opposed to narrative, self-expression,
the reader, along with the poetic "I" of the text, enters into a new
"moment" of being.
   A final observation on the style of Clarice Lispector, which is as
famous in Brazilian letters as it is identifiable, has to do with the
nature and function of paradox in her work. As it is generally
understood in literature and philosophy, a paradox involves a statement that, though appearing to make no sense or to be self-contradictory, actually makes a valid, noncontradictory point. In *The
Well-Wrought Urn* (1947) Cleanth Brooks argues that, defined in a
larger sense of the term, paradox emerges as the real language of

poetry, of a poetic conception of self and of life.[12] If we accept this expanded definition of paradox, one that would include our understanding of the term as a rhetorical figure as well as a concept involving a certain kind of authorial attitude, we can see how paradox would play a key role in Lispector's lyrically and philosophically oriented fictional world. Paradox, then, is important to our understanding not only of how Lispector writes (paradox seen as a rhetorical figure, an aspect of her overall style) but of what she writes about (her personal conception of what the real human experience is like). In writing this way, Lispector's style often combines two or more terms that in ordinary language usage seem to be contrary in meaning. As a poetical writer, however, Lispector turns these apparently contradictory couplings into oxymorons, an old form of poetic (especially Elizabethan love poetry and religious poetry, two modes of expression that are fundamental to Lispector's work) conceit that allows a writer to verbalize the inconsistencies, contradictions, and complexities of the human condition at the same instant that he gives credence to the truth of their existence. Thus, Lispector's sense of paradox is both thematic and formal. She sees the oddities and incongruities of human reality and reproduces them by means of creating paradoxical situations, which, because they have the feel of real life to them, slowly come to imbue her stories and novels with a strong sense of violence (emotional rather than physical) and absurdity. The essence of paradox in Lispector's fictive world is that while her narratives seem "unrealistic" or "antimimetic" in that they are largely cerebral and illustrative of inner divagation, they are actually quite "realistic." This is so, Lispector would say, because the human experience is more truthfully and more fully explained by focusing on the paradoxical, inconsistent, and often self-contradictory inner world than by any presentation of what acts we commit in the three-dimensional world of people in action. In sum, the famous style of Clarice Lispector is a direct reflection of the understanding and confusion, the loquaciousness and silence, and the love and hate that coexist constantly and simultaneously in each of us and most vividly define our human condition. In a very real way, as Assis Brasil demonstrates in *Clarice Lispector,* to understand Lispector's style is to understand Clarice Lispector and her view of the world.

The Structuring of the
Lispectorian Lyrical Novel

The lyrical novel, which, as Clarice Lispector writes it, falls into
the category of the open novel, involves the transformation of characterization, plotting, and scenic depiction into patterns of imagery.
Lispector's fiction tends to illustrate her attitudes concerning reality,
consciousness, and knowledge and it is her portrayal of the epistemological process that characterizes her literary work as being a
fusion of narrative and poetry. Freedman's tripartite concept of the
lyrical novel's composition calls our attention to the importance that
structure and design have in the Lispectorian version of this form:[13]
first, the immediate portrayal of the theme through images, scenes,
or symbolic figures without the intervention of a universe of action
and characterization means that theme is made manifest by imagery
(isolated and collective) and metaphor (including paradox and am-
bivalence) rather than by action or traditional modes of characterization; second, by rearranging the narrative sequences to reflect
directly a pattern of images in which the author's personal (poetic)
vision is expressed to the reader, the lyrical novel involves a manipulation of the ordering of the various scenes in the story so as
to reflect better its imagery (form) and theme (content); third, the
implementation of a central protagonist in such a work to act as a
focus for the perceptions that reflect the experiences and thoughts
that the work as a whole seeks to translate into a cohesive, organic
pattern means that this central protagonist must be acutely self-
reflective, like the lyrical "I" in poetry. This central character reflects
(or is the locus for) the main themes that the novel attempts to
portray. Whatever the lyrical novel is "about" will be reflected in
the form of the protagonist; it is this figure that gives the poetic
heart to the remainder of the novel. The protagonist of the lyrical
novel is both the catalyst that sets other forces in motion and the
adhesive that binds them all together into a single, coordinated
unit. Thus, when we speak of the "meaning" of *Perto do coração
selvagem, Água viva, O lustre,* or *A cidade sitiada,* for example, we
should not attempt to concentrate our attention upon the meanings
that emerge from the words as much as upon our responses to the
relationships that evolve among the various juxtaposed portions of
the work, the intertextualities involved. The meaning, therefore,

of this type of novel may be said to lie among the interstices of the structure.[14]

The circular structure of works such as *A maçã no escuro, A paixão segundo G. H., Uma aprendizagem,* and *Água viva* brings to mind what Sharon Spencer calls the most common pattern of movement in the achitectonic (or open) novel.[15] Martim's ironic return to the very society he had earlier fled and the fact the G. H. faces the dawn of another day after having experienced a devastating mystical revelation both indicate how far, structurally, Lispector had progressed with these later novels. Nevertheless, her novelistic innovativeness between 1961 and 1977 is not without precedent, since in *Perto do coração selvagem,* her first work, we see considerable experimentation with scenic juxtaposition, fragmented characterizations, and temporal dislocation. In the first three novels, however, events, often seemingly trivial, banal, and without significance, could be charted as points along a line. F. G. Reis, in fact, believes that Lispector's fiction is essentially linear in nature.[16] This line of action, however, never reflects rising and falling action in the Aristotelian sense; rather, the "line of action," the plot, is, for Clarice Lispector, open-ended, uncertain, and suggestive of various interpretations. This strongly suggests that as early as 1942 (when she was composing *Perto do coração selvagem*) Clarice Lispector was concerned with the issues that would many years later become known as the "antinovel" or "new novel" movement.

The structural innovations so startlingly apparent in *Água viva,* then, are rooted not just in *A maçã no escuro* but reach all the way back to *Perto do coração selvagem.* Adonias Filho, in fact, has observed that this book marks Lispector's first attempt to renovate Brazilian prose fiction in terms of language and structure,[17] two concerns that continue to be vital to any understanding of her fiction. In terms of its structuring, her first novel appears rather crude when contrasted to the subtle forms at play in *Água viva* or *A paixão segundo G. H.,* but nevertheless it is clear that Lispector is as much preoccupied with the manner in which her tale is presented as with the essence of the tale itself. The self-consciousness of Lispector's later work also attests to her concern with the interrelationship of form and content.

The retrograde structural design of *Perto do coração selvagem* reflects the story of Joana as she progresses, emotionally and intellectually, from small child to adult woman. Mundane on the surface, this tale generates a unique potency by means of the deeply personal but largely unconscious ebb and flow of consciousness that characterize the protagonist and reflect the emotive spirit of lyric poetry. It is only in a superficial sense that this novel loses contact with the tangibility of human existence; quite to the contrary, it actually comes to grips thematically with those deep-seated anxieties that characterize so much of the human experience: solitude, the inability to communicate, frustration, fear, confusion, and doubt. In dealing with such subjects Lispector finds it more expeditious to give her novel a fluid, nonrigid structure, one that will not only permit her to plumb the depths of her protagonist's mercurial consciousness but a structure that will actually enhance and even reflect it. Álvaro Lins praises Clarice Lispector for her skill in analyzing human passions, the audacity of her efforts, and the vitality of her style, but he also believes that in the second half of this novel, which he judges to be too vague and indistinct, she becomes trapped in her own labyrinth.[18] This, for Lins, would explain why, as he sees it, the novel ends in an incomplete or fragmentary fashion, a feature of Lispector's work that we now see as fully characteristic of it. One must ask, however, if, given Lispector's thematic concerns, it was not her aesthetic intention to make the book conclude open-endedly so that the reader is left with the impression that the reality in which he has just participated is "real," that human reality is "really" a process of growth, of becoming, of change. *Perto do coração selvagem,* like Lispector's final novel, *Um sopro de vida,* ends as a lyric poem might, that is, inconclusively in terms of any logically ordered sequence of events (plot) but conclusively in terms of the emotional experience undergone (one person's response to the issues of human existence).

In *Perto do coração selvagem* we move directly and rather abruptly from the view (and image) of a little girl to that of a married woman, one who is jolted into a reconsideration of her life because of a sudden realization that her existence is a farce. This shift in perspective and tone parallels a marked change in the psychological development of the central character, Joana. And, as Assis Brasil has noted,[19] this abrupt jump becomes "organic" in terms of the relationship between form and content in the novel. The structure of even this first, sometimes unsubtle novel mirrors the author's concern for the nature of the creative process itself, a concern that evidences a belief in the absolute need for a naturally developing unity in every art object.

Thus the then (in 1944) startling, temporally dislocated structure of *Perto do coração selvagem* reflected Lispector's awareness of her own need, and of the need in Brazilian literature, for a new, more vital narrative form, a new mode of novelistic expression. Hence her desire to merge form and content, design and theme, into a self-generating, nondivisible unit, antedated Asturias's *El señor presidente* (1946) by two years and represents the kind of prose fiction that Ralph Freedman, years later, would describe as the lyrical novel. Clarice Lispector, then, should be given credit for having been among the very earliest structural and stylistic reformers of the novel form in Latin America, for being an authentic forerunner of the justly famous "new novel" of Spanish America.

Point of View

Remembering that one of the most basic questions concerning method in the craft of fiction is point of view, the place in which the narrator stands in relation to the story, we know that, broadly speaking, there are basically four points of view that can be used in a story: omniscient, limited omniscient, first person, and dramatic. There are, of course, virtually endless variations on these, but inevitably the problem of point of view deals with the manner in which the narrator transmits his tale to the reader.[20] When analyzing fiction, in terms of point of view, we must necessarily deal with such questions as these: who speaks to the reader, author, characters, or, ostensibly, no one? From what position or angle does the teller or commentator present the tale? Is he involved in it or is he an "objective" observer? How does the teller speak to the reader? Does he use the real author's words, thoughts, perceptions, feelings, or those of some other character, and how far removed is the teller of the tale from the crux of the story? What effect does this distance have on the story?[21] Because of its focus on language as both subject and instrument, Lispector's fiction offers much to readers interested in current narratological theory and criticism, an approach to her art that has so far been neglected.

But while these general questions may be applied to Lispector's fiction, there are certain unique characteristics of her work that must be considered if we are fully and properly to appreciate how she handles the role of point of view. The lyrical process, as it manifests itself in the medium of the Lispectorian novel, tends to expand in scope because the center of awareness, like the passive, lyrical "I" of poetry, is also an experiencing protagonist. Hence, as Freedman observes, "the poet's stance is turned into an epistemological act."[22] The point of view in such novels is necessarily hermetic and interior; protagonists such as Martim, G. H., Lóri, Ana, and the voices of *Água viva* and *Um sopro de vida* are all profoundly self-reflective and, at the same time, also engaged in a continuous examination of their own perception of the world. What these characters think, feel, and do is reproduced less as a reflection of a knowable, quantitative universe, one that can be expressed linguistically in the subject/ verb/object form, than as an ongoing, free-flowing system of imagery and speculation. In *A maçã no escuro,* for example, the imagery centers upon the motifs of darkness, silence, isolation, and desolation. This is why a close reading of Clarice Lispector's fiction shows it to be very similar to lyrical poetry, especially in the manner in which it dissolves realities external to their inner beings and then re-creates, or restructures them into a poetrylike form. Martim's point of view in *A maçã no escuro* establishes the parameters of the entire novel and also functions as the predominant device by which the world surrounding Martim's mind is translated not into cause and effect, action-oriented relationships but into patterns of subverbal, associative imagery. In *A paixão segundo G. H.,* to cite another example, the restricted point of view of G. H. prevents her from entering into any communication with anyone other than the various mercurial aspects of her own evolving being.

In all of Lispector's novels, in fact, communication, while it exists as a basic, recurring theme, does not usually take place on any meaningful level between people. In Lispector's world ". . . communication is sometimes difficult, especially when the forms are too private or too strained in their meanings."[23] The intensely private world reflected in the dominant point of view, almost invariably that of the protagonist, makes it seem that the person who "tells" the story is also the person most centrally involved in the action. The point of view, shifting subtly from omniscient to first person and often to third person as well, becomes the major shaping force in Lispector's narratives. In *Água viva,* for example, the dominant point of view is that of a nameless persona who is a combination of narrator and protagonist. The action of this novel, which centers on a silent investigation into the essence of the artistic act and its connection to self-affirmation, is overwhelmingly mental. The organic unity of self and world in *Água viva* in many ways is the apex of the direction in which Lispector had been heading since her initial novel. This unity, held together by the speculation of Lispector's lyrical "I," dictates the form that the accompanying imagery in each story will take. This is accomplished by altering the manner in which the self, or "I," perceives itself and the outer world. In doing so, the narrative voice of Lispector's fiction is similar to the "voice" of a lyrical poem. It is through this "I" or self, therefore, that Lispector's narratives gain their unique tone and considerable emotive power.

But in Lispector's fiction, and especially in her novels, the conflict develops in accordance with the particular point of view employed. The structure of such a book as *Água viva,* for example, or even *Perto do coração selvagem,* or *A cidade sitiada,* is determined primarily by the manner in which the story unfolds, which itself is controlled by the dominant point of view. In *Perto do coração selvagem,* Joana, the protagonist, is a composite figure, an analogy between the lyrical "I" of verse poetry and the hero figure in traditional prose fiction. And since the formal presentation of a self involves a self-reflexive method, most fiction of the type Lispector writes requires a single point of view.[24] This "self-reflexive" quality is clearly present in all of Lispector's fiction; each of her protagonists, her lyrical "I's," engages in constant self-analysis.

Lispector, however, does not limit herself to a single point of view in constructing her fictional world. She alternates between a third person that is both omniscient and limited and first-person interior monologues or "silent soliloquies." Lispector, not content with describing things or with delineating the length, width, and breadth of the physical world, narrates from within by plunging deep into the human psyche to examine the relationships between people and the world of objects that surround them. This strongly phenomenological relationship gives rise to a strong presence of objectivity in her different points of view and is reminiscent of the French *nouveau roman.*

In terms of characterization an obvious effect of using the interior monologue technique is that characters are never firm or "completed"; they are in flux, forever fragmentary, and not necessarily what they appear to be from the outside. This situation, of course, must ultimately lead to an expression of those chaotic thought impulses that lie nearest—and even within—the subconscious. What we know, therefore, about Lispector's characters is essentially what we know about the "lyric I" in a poem; we know what he or she is thinking (or what is "randomly" running through the mind) and feeling (usually an ever-changing bundle of contradictory sensations). Moreover, we approach Lispector's characters in the same way that we approach the central consciousness in a lyric poem. We know little other than what we feel and think, but this is enough, and, as Lispector constantly suggests, it may well be more than anyone can control. In Lispector's novels and stories, as in lyric poetry, the action tends to be one of a subjective, inwardly directed nature. Typically her narratives are structured on the Joycean concept of the epiphany rather than on "realistic" sequences of action and event. In Lispector's fiction we see less and less of what a character does, for he "does" very little, but we learn much from what he says, how he reacts to outside stimuli, and from what he thinks.[25] Much modern poetry takes its form from this same type of dramatic monologue and so it does not surprise us that Clarice Lispector, a lyrically inspired narrativist, is intensely concerned with language, its structure, its connection to "reality," and its reliability as a communicative medium. Her dramatic monologues come alive when a protagonist such as Virgínia, Lóri, Lucrécia, Joana, or Mrs. Jorge B. Xavier ("A procura de una dignidade" [The search for a dignity]) divests herself of all the usual psychic trappings of a normal human being and attempts a confrontation with the truth of her solitary being. It is at this point, when she is struggling to verbalize her innermost problems, thoughts, and sensations, that Lispector shows her greatest skill as a creative writer. As Álvaro Lins says of the author and her linguistic concerns, "her most effective recourse is the interior monologue, and the reconstruction of thought in words."[26]

Lispector's preoccupation with language, as a medium of artistic communication and as a philosophical problem about the nature of existence,[27] is closely linked to the manner in which her protagonists view themselves and their world, but it also has far-reaching consequences in terms of character development. Lispector's characters are locked into themselves, silently struggling to decipher their feelings and thoughts. They are like actors standing silently on a stage, hardly ever speaking to anyone but afraid to vent their true feelings, anxious that the words they choose may distort their intentions. When they do attempt to communicate some messages to other beings, they are doomed to failure and their hopelessly subjective, fragmented, contradictory utterances resist any clarifying interpretation. Like much modern poetry, the real merit of Lispector's characters' words is that they simply "are"; they exist—and must be allowed to remain—in their own private context. If, as García Márquez suggests in *Cien años de soledad,* history imposes a kind of solitude on people, language achieves a similar end for the characters of Clarice Lispector. Her characters' plight—their isolation and their inability to communicate—is constantly set off by the clash between their dialogues and their monologues. Nevertheless, as Massaud Moisés notes, there is common ground between these two modes of expression. There is an

obvious similarity between the interior monologues and the dialogues in the fiction of Clarice Lispector: we are always dealing with a monologue of the "I" adversed to itself, apparently addressed to an "other" who, in turn concentrates on enunciating his own existential drama.[28]

It is typically Lispector's intention to catch a mind in moments of insight or discovery, to isolate and then alternate those moments in which her characters see, or think they see, life as it really is. These minds are usually close to the center of the novel's conflict, and the recording of their "moments of awareness" or "insight" provides the building blocks of Clarice Lispector's fiction, the perspectives from which she wants the reader to enter her stories. It is the shifting, metaphorically rendered consciousness of each of her protagonists that binds each novel and story together and gives it its pattern and design. It is therefore not surprising that Lispector adopts points of view that allow her to focus not only upon what goes on in the mind of her main character, but upon how other people in the story, people not privy to the inner turmoil, either misinterpret what is happening to the protagonist or disregard it completely. Either way the effect is to isolate the protagonist totally, to show him or her sentenced to a state of eternal solitude.

The protagonist's point of view, limited though it is in terms of what it can say about what other people do, say, think, or feel, provides, then, the structural basis for each of her novels. And since Lispector does not write fiction in which an action-oriented plot reigns supreme, she does not have to be concerned with her central character's ability or inability to know for certain what is going on. *A maçã no escuro,* for example, a vague novel full of stops and starts and extraneous fragments of narrative that reflect the digressive nature of human thought, ends as indecisively as it begins. The novel offers a minimum of physical action, but for approximately 350 pages the reader does witness a reenactment of a venerable Lispector theme—the development of a human consciousness and its quest for self-awareness and knowledge. In general, Lispector assumes this same Bildungsroman stance in all her other novels. Whether it is an intensely human character like Joana, Ana, or a "voice" without body or name, as in *Água viva,* some isolated, self-reflexive awareness forms the heart of her fiction. In each case, the dominant point of view is that of the character most involved in the conflict, the one who will give the author the most freedom in expressing these states of awareness.

It must also be remembered, however, that the primary artistic feature of Lispector's use of point of view is that even though she concentrates on depicting the various levels of consciousness of a single character, she constantly makes subtle shifts in her dominant point of view in order to manipulate more effectively the manner in which she wishes to relate to the issue, the growth of awareness, that she is presenting. We feel empathy for Lispector's characters not so much for what they say, but because other people around them ignore or disregard them or misconstrue so badly what they say. And it is Lispector's unobtrusive shifting of point of view that achieves this end, this presentation of the protagonist as he sees himself from the inside and as he is seen by others from the outside. Because Lispector is necessarily concerned with the reader's response to her characters, she also tries to reproduce in her reader's mind the same spark of insight that she strikes in her protagonists. This helps explain why her novels are so taxing; they require the reader to participate actively and intensely in the development of her protagonist's mind, much as a lyric poem. Lispector's point of view, therefore, often assumes a dramatic pose, or mode, one that tends to imply more than it states. [29]

As the central consciousness of their lyrical fictions, Lispector's protagonists also reflect a creative process that is, to a certain extent, bound up in Lispector's own psyche. Her novels are intensely private, and, at times (as in *Um sopro de vida* or *A hora da estrela*), seemingly even autobiographical. But even so, they seldom fail to project an inescapable universality. Because the point of view in Lispector's fiction is typically interiorized, the reader seems to be "eavesdropping" on the flow of information that runs through a character's mind. The syntax is frequently jumbled and thoughts are more often expressed in terms of symbols and metaphors than by any ostensibly denotative or analytical language use. Lispector's consistent objective in terms of point of view is to dramatize the flux in mental states and to show how these are ultimately not knowable by other people. Depending on how deeply into the psychic realm one plunges, the more the logic and syntax of normal, rational discourse begins to disappear and the more the associational polysemy of language as symbolic system begins to take over. This explains why long passages of works such as *Água viva* or *Um sopro de vida* strike the reader as poetry even before he realizes their narrative function in a work of fiction, even lyrical fiction. Lispector's protagonists actually say very little, though they ruminate endlessly, and so their stories are composed primarily of disconnected thoughts, unspoken words, images, recollections, and dreams. When they do speak aloud, their words seem to have little bearing on what has been going through their minds. In this respect Lispector's characters exhibit concerns that remind one of the "alternity" in language use that George Steiner discusses in *After Babel*.[30] Clarice Lispector's central characters, from Joana through Martim and up to the voices in *Água viva* and *Um sopro de vida*, all function as both protagonists and narrators. As such they express lyrically a flow of their own private, tangled thoughts, feelings, and perceptions, and their angle of vision, or point of view, is inevitably that of a fixed center, that of the "lyrical I." In *A paixão segundo G. H.*, for example, any serious consideration of the nature of the character of G. H. must be integrally linked to the larger question of point of view, how and why G. H. tells her own story.

But as we have seen, Lispector does not assume a single, unvarying point of view, although a superficial reading of her work can leave one with that impression. She constantly shifts the focus in subtle, complex ways, and is even capable of striking two or three slightly different points of view within the same paragraph or the same sentence. For example, in *A maçã no escuro* she continually shifts from general omniscience to protagonist/narrator (or the "eye-witness") to multiple selective omniscience. In this important novel

Lispector is concerned with the way in which personality and circumstances impinge upon the sensibilities of three distinct yet similar people. Their stories are interlocking and profoundly intertwined, and are reminiscent, in different ways, of *Nightwood* (1937), *The Waves* (1931), *To the Lighthouse* (1927), and *As I Lay Dying* (1930). Lispector's notion of point of view tends to run strongly in the direction of scene, both inside the mind and in the world external to it. The shift from normal omniscience (in which Clarice Lispector peers in and then proceeds to describe for the reader what is going on in her characters' minds) to multiple selective omniscience (wherein the reader is simply shown what is going on in a character's mind, without authorial commentary) keeps the point of view hermetic and interior but also allows for a sharper focus and thereby heightens the dramatic intensity of the various scenes. This weaving in and out of a character's always-changing stream of consciousness—sometimes with authorial guidance and explanation but often without— demands close attention and involvement on the reader's part. In *A paixão segundo G. H.*, *Água viva*, and *Um sopro de vida*, Lispector allows the mind of a single protagonist to develop itself, something she became more skilled at doing the more she wrote. Aesthetically, this issue is particularly interesting in regard to the self-conscious and confessional *Um sopro de vida*.

In general, then, point of view for Clarice Lispector provides more flexible storytelling technique than a casual reading of her work might suggest. The shifts are many and subtle, and yet an overall atmosphere of hermeticism, silence, and solitude is maintained throughout the development of her narratives. As with other lyrical fiction, Lispector's central characters are always seen in a dual role, that of the observer (their "subjectivity") and the observed (their "objective" being). They are intensely thoughtful, sensitive, and contemplative, but when it comes to verbalizing their thoughts they are curiously not inarticulate but inexpressive; when they speak out loud, they seem fearful, or perhaps merely hesitant to organize and utter their innermost thoughts and feelings. The words they speak do not seem to express the tormenting jumble of thoughts that best characterizes their psychic existences. Whenever they are forced to leave the silent solipsism of their inner existences and speak the language of everyday human discourse, a great sense of failure, frustration, and isolation engulfs them. That they come to know this intuitively or rationally accounts for the sense of frustration and anxiety that is so endemic to Lispector's fiction. It is a tribute to her skill at handling point of view that she so effectively treads this shaky ground between her characters' free-floating, silent interior monologues and their spoken words, their conversations, and their discussions of social phenomena. This aspect of Lispector's art is strongly apparent in *A hora da estrela*. By varying her point of view, Lispector allows the reader to experience the protagonist's private inner world as well as his public, outer world. By establishing these two general perspectives, by merging them, and by constantly contrasting them, Lispector uses point of view to impart an unexpectedly human sense of verisimilitude to her fiction.

Dialogue, Monologue, and the Stream of Consciousness

Dialogue, the actual words characters speak to each other, has a dramatic structural function similar to that of description, that is, it helps satisfy the reader's desire for concreteness, for facts, for certitude. Lispector's attempt to resolve the conflicts that she sees as existing between existence and a linguistic expression of it as well as someone's comprehension of the entire process necessarily involves the problem of words and the manner in which they relate to the subject being presented and to the subject doing the presenting. Clarice Lispector felt compelled, as Wittgenstein had said, "to speak of that which obliges us to be silent," and it is in this sense that we come to understand and appreciate the constant structural antagonism between silence (mental flow, associations, and imagery) and sound (verbalized words and dialogue) that exists in her novels.

Lispector's descriptive language is much richer, much more subtle and full of nuance than her dialogue, which is spare, stark, and seemingly disjointed, although it nevertheless succeeds quite well in performing the three major functions of dialogue: (1) it imparts information to the reader and to the characters (although in Lispector's world the words used may not always convey accurate information since a character may be mistaken, misinformed, lying, or merely striking an "ironic" pose); (2) it reveals multiple levels of psychic tension (this being in addition to character or personality development); and (3) it helps advance the plot (speeches for Lispector occupy a unique but integral part of development from conflict to plot to resolution. It is the contrast between spoken dialogue and the unspoken interior monologue that must be carefully observed in this sense). Dialogue, while often telling much about the speaker's outlook on life, is generally consistent with his or her characterization. The character's true personality should be at least partially revealed in dialogue and in so doing dialogue contributes to the coherence and "believability" of the work. But, it is often said, good dialogue is not really a mimicking of the way "real people" speak; it is much more selective, carefully pruned and controlled so as to project other, more subtle aspects of a character's state of mind. Not surprisingly, this is where Lispector's utilization of irony is most clearly perceived.

In general, however, dialogue is not a dominant aspect of Lispector's prose, although when it is used it succeeds quite well in illustrating the great chasm that separates what we think we are saying from what we are really saying, or from the way other people are interpreting our words. With the exception of *Uma aprendizagem ou o livro dos prazeres,* when dialogue does appear in Lispector's work it equates less and less well with what Lispector's characters really want to say. The spoken word, oddly sterile, is portrayed as slipping further and further from any controlling connection with the impulses of the inner world. In *O lustre,* for example, dialogue is cryptic, evasive, and vague; its meaning is either so trivial as to be inconsequential or it must be treated as a cipher to be decoded.[31] The style of Lispector's dialogue is very close to her general descriptive style, but there is a curious uniqueness about the way her dialogue fits, often with ironic implications, into her overall narration. One realizes that Lispector is attempting a kind of simultaneity by projecting her characters through a labyrinth of self-speculation but having them uttering bits and pieces of thought that may be taken as being either lightly conversational or profoundly philosophical, depending on the nature of the circumstances. The obtuse non sequiturs that dot Lispector's prose stem from this ironically contraposed simultaneity of thought and expression, all of which reinforces the thematic ambiguity of her work as well.

The reader responds to this admixture of "spoken" and nonspoken language by experiencing Lispector's characters in three ways: (1) verbally, by means of words that are often common to the point of being meaningless but are sometimes taken as being enigmatic and charged with unexpected meanings; (2) rationally thoughtful, when the characters silently ponder the meaning of human existence and their place in the world; and (3) irrationally associational, when Lispector attempts to capture linguistically the essence of her characters' free-floating, subconscious, jumbled thought patterns. One becomes quickly dazzled by the weaving of Lispector's relentless psychic meanderings, a weaving which gives form to the deeply rooted archetypal bases of her characters. But often when the reader encounters some lines of dialogue exchanged by Lispector's characters, it is like being rudely awakened from a deep, dream-filled slumber. The reader is jarred, confused, and cannot always tell what the meaning of the words are; they may pertain to an incident, a word, or a "look" that took place several pages earlier, or to some psychic state, "real" or imagined, that may be only partially understood by the speaker himself. There is also a recurrent use of the utterance that "does not follow" the dialogues with which it seems to be associated. Characters suddenly say things that do not seem to have any immediate relation to any other utterances or situations. Structurally, these utterances become issues of temporal signification and represent an attempt by the author to show how verbalized words, aside from whatever meaning or significance we choose to give them, express only the surface moment of our conscious minds. Once uttered, moreover, they become the property of other moments and other consciousnesses as much as of the speakers; the essential privacy of languages is both defiled and extended. Words are only the tip of the iceberg, so to speak, and it is the submerged, evolving mass that lives inside each person that most concerns Clarice Lispector.

For Lispector it is dialogue that allows her to place into sharp relief her belief that words, wholly symbolic in function (and therefore subject to interpretation rather than definition), form only the uppermost layer of human consciousness, and that the words most people speak often have little or nothing to do with the tangled web that they are really thinking and feeling. Words are treacherous entities for Lispector, yet they are also the key to understanding her art.[32] For Lispector, words are the only mechanism we have for approaching the ontological problems of reality—what is it, how do we know, and, finally, what is the nature of our relationship to it? Hence they play a crucial role in the development of her narratives. Human communication, or more precisely the lack of it, is a theme that is central to any understanding of Lispector's work, and it is a theme that arises from her concept of words as a communicative medium related directly to the nature of one's being. The often glaring conflict between dialogue and the unspoken, often even unconceptualized word, lends Lispector's fiction a very unique, unmistakable quality, and it is no accident or stylistic quirk that her characters say the things they do.

This ongoing, discontinuity between the spoken and unspoken word may be further contrasted if we consider it as existing between spoken dialogue and the silent interior monologue. It has long been suggested that the "silent monologue" would actually be a more accurate translation of the French term *monologue interieur* and that it would more faithfully suggest the true nature of the original term. The interior monologue, first employed by Édouard Dujardin in his *Les Lauriers sont coupés* (1877), is a literary term that refers to a technique, to an unspoken discourse, one presented "directly" (as in the Molly Bloom soliloquy of *Ulysses*) or "indirectly," as in many of the novels of Virginia Woolf. Stream of consciousness, on the other hand, is commonly used to refer to a certain kind of subject matter, and a tapping of several levels of the mental process. Although the interior monologue, as a narrative device at least, is considerably older than the notion that stream of consciousness more properly involves subject matter, ever since Joyce, Proust, and Woolf readers have tended to lump them together and overlook their distinctive features and their separate evolutions. Because both these terms are important to any study of the structure and design of Lispector's fiction, they deserve close attention.

Scholes and Kellogg believe that the interior monologue in narrative literature is a

direct, immediate presentation of the unspoken thoughts of a character without any intervening narrator. Like direct discourse or dialogue it is a dramatic element in narrative literature, but it can be present only in narrative because only in narrative can a soliloquy remain unspoken and yet be understood by an audience.[33]

These same critics then go on to say that the term "stream of consciousness" is most often used to designate

any presentation in literature of the illogical, ungrammatical, mainly associative patterns of human thought. Such thoughts may be spoken or unspoken. As a literary phenomenon, stream-of-consciousness is of fairly late development, with its most obvious roots in Lockean theory of the workings of the mind and Sterne's adaptation of Locke in *Tristram Shandy*.[34]

These two features, the interior monologue technique and the use of stream-of-consciousness subject matter, dominate the novels of Clarice Lispector. Their presence is felt even in her initial novel in 1944, but by *Água viva*, in 1973, the interior monologue especially has, with variations, become her dominant mode of expression. Lispector's protagonists, from Joana of *Perto do coração selvagem* to the voice of *Um sopro de vida*, all engage in lengthy and ceaselessly flowing silent monologues; only rarely do they attempt to utter their thoughts out loud.

But these unspoken monologues actually assume the dramatic significance of formal soliloquies and, as such, succeed for Lispector in transforming all the technical formalities of the traditional novel into the formal prose poetry of the lyrical novel. Just as in Woolf's *The Waves* or Barnes's *Nightwood*, where the formal soliloquies convert the traditional, realistic novel into a kind of prose poetry, so, too, do Joana, Martim, G. H., and Ana convert both the "inner" and "outer" worlds into a single, poetic design. Freedman, commenting on the peculiar manner in which the soliloquy (or interior monologue) relates to the lyrical novel, writes:

soliloquies are of necessity interior, but as poetry they serve an additional purpose. They are the *forms* in which moments—the meeting of association and memory with the facts of the external world—are caught to reflect content and coherence in lyrical narrative. They act as units, both lyrical and dramatic, to supply the instances of perception and recognition of which the novels are composed.[35]

Freedman's words have a particular significance for Lispector's novels. Since her work deals so consistently with "moments," fleeting instances of awareness, and cognition in which she must demonstrate this "meeting of association and memory with the facts of the external world," these same moments must, by necessity, come to dominate the formal design of her novels. These moments of awareness, or epiphanies, which compose the basic structure of such novels as *O lustre* or *A cidade sitiada* or *Perto do coração selvagem* and such stories as "Love," "Family Ties," and "The Dinner," serve to unify both the form and the content of the work. The interior monologues—the soliloquies—are the mediums that transform themselves into the poetic forms that ultimately give shape to Lispector's fictions.

The interior monologue, we know, really has two forms: (1) the "direct," in which the author does not seem to be present and in which the character's inner self is revealed directly to the reader, as if the latter were overhearing a conversation in which the character's words were being uttered; and (2) the "indirect," in which the author clearly seems to be present, even to the point of functioning as selector, presenter, guide, and commentator. Clarice Lispector makes use of both techniques. She often begins a scene by having her omniscient third-person narrator declare that someone felt a certain way, but then she quickly slides into the direct interior monologue and the articulation of the stream of thought and feeling that surges through her character's conscious and unconscious mind. Finally, she might offer someone's reaction to the silent discourse just presented. Lispector consistently works this way in order to trace and reconstruct the internal emotional and intellectual experience of her protagonists on any single level or on any combinations of levels of consciousness. She may at one moment show how verbalized words—dialogue—seem to rise to the top of our minds, like bubbles that rise to the surface of a pond and burst, or, as in *A paixão segundo G. H.*, she may reach downward to the nonverbalized level, where images must be used to represent the tangle of nonverbalized sensations and emotions that exist there. Because of the nature of Lispector's essential subject matter—consciousness and awareness—the form that she employs to present her content must necessarily appear to be unrestricted, uncensored, often illogical, and free of the preconceived interpretations that arise from following conventional patterns of syntax. This explains why Lispector's fiction is so taxing; although the words she uses are "simple" ones, the way she assembles them, her syntax, challenges our ability to interpret, construct, or deconstruct their meanings properly. Her "opaqueness," or ambiguity, derives from this unusual patterning of her sentences and the responses they generate.

The close interrelationship between form and content in Lispector's novels has not escaped the eyes of certain Brazilian critics. Adonias Filho, for example, thinks that the monologue form carries with it certain thematic implications, especially involving the "confession" (or the "lyric I"), but that its real importance lies in its structural significance.[36] Such an observation also tends to substantiate the idea that Lispector was not only in the vanguard of the new novel in Brazil, but in Spanish America as well. Essentially, what Filho is arguing is that the interior monologue, direct and indirect, ultimately provides the predominant structure of Lispector's fiction, the basic theme of which is perception, the depicting of the moment of awareness and self-realization. Characters such as Lucrécia, Virgínia, Lóri, G. H., and Martim all demonstrate how, for Clarice Lispector, the interior monologue functions as a kind of weather vane, a device by which the winds of psychological ebb and flow can be charted.

Chapter Four
Novels and Stories

Perto do coração selvagem (1944)

This first novel, the writing of which actually began in 1942, is composed of two parts. Part 1, divided into nine chapters, operates on two different but interrelated planes, one concerning the childhood of the protagonist, Joana, and one concerning her adulthood. Part 2 of the novel concerns itself primarily with Joana's slow realization of who and what she is. Specifically, it focuses on the social, sexual, and psychological complexities of a triangular "love" relationship involving Joana, a frustrated middle-class urban woman, Otávio, her unfaithful husband, and Lídia, Otávio's pregnant ex-fiancée. Joana learns of her husband's infidelity and challenges him about it. Otávio then departs and Joana feels herself "free" in ways she had never before experienced. The novel ends with a long interior monologue in which we see Joana seemingly about to make a new life for herself, based on a newly "authentic" identity but a life even Joana senses to be full of danger, disappointment, and potential failure.

The first part of the novel is dominated by flashback scenes and experiences that give partial form to Joana's childhood but that make no attempt to explain or analyze it. These experiences, which show how Joana is aware, though in a confused way, of being both an observer and a participant, include the following: the urge to have a close relationship with her father, who was a writer; becoming an orphan; intimate conversations with a teacher for whom she feels a desperate "love"; sensing an aversion toward the middle-class aunt who adopts her; stealing a book; the sensuousness (and symbolism) of the sea and her bath; the emotional and physical crisis of puberty; and the discovery of her own body (an early and necessary step in her progression toward a later psychological self-realization).

Interspersed with these scenes of childhood experiences are other scenes that show Joana as an adult. We see her in a conventional marriage to Otávio, in her daily routine and in her moments of measured happiness and sadness. In addition, however, we also see her "talking" with a mysterious *mulher da voz* ("woman of the voice"), whose ideas about life, existence, and self-awareness have a powerful if uncertain effect on Joana. The final chapter of part 1, "Otávio," focuses on her husband and ties together the two planes of development in part 1, Joana's childhood experiences and those of her adult life.

Part 2 shows how introspective and reflective Joana, now an adult and trapped in a servile and meaningless life, has become. This introspectiveness dominates Joana's development as a character and, by the novel's uncertain conclusion (when she seems ready to undertake a new life), establishes her as the prototype for Lispector's later protagonists.

The catalyst for all the "action" in the second part is Joana's unsatisfactory marriage to Otávio, a man who remains essentially an unknown entity to her and to whom she is attracted and by whom she is repelled. In a way that parallels her conflicting feelings for Otávio, Joana herself is torn between her impulse toward self-affirming action and acquiescence to her social role as an urban middle-class wife. She attempts to vent her frustration through artistic creation, but this only serves to frustrate her even more. The ever-increasing inner tension suffered by Joana is exacerbated because her husband, aware that Joana knows about his affair, chooses to act as if nothing were wrong. The falsity—or, in Sartrean terms, the "inauthenticity" of this situation—proves too much for Joana to bear, and she separates both from her husband and from the "lover" she had rather diffidently secured for herself. The internalized tension of the last part of the novel culminates in a long interior monologue by Joana. This monologue, which recalls the Molly Bloom soliloquy at the end of *Ulysses,* equates the third-person narrative voice with Joana and shows how she is attempting to assume responsibility for her own life and being. Showing a hitherto unknown strength and resolve (but still aware of facing an unknown and threatening world), Joana's mind, caught in the process of "becoming," thinks:

Viverei maior do que na infância, serei brutal e mal feita como uma pedra, serei leve e vaga como o que se sente e não se entende, . . . nada impedirá meu caminho até a morte-sem-medo, de qualquer luta ou descanso me levantarei forte e bela como um cavalo nôvo.[1]

(I shall live even more completely than in childhood, I shall be brutal and half made like a stone, I shall be light and vague like what one feels but does not understand . . . nothing will block my path toward the death-without-fear, and whether it be from battle or repose I shall rise up strong and beautiful, like a newly born horse.)

As this passage indicates, Lispector does not engage in psychological analysis. She records the psychological experience of her characters, their thought flow, but makes no effort to explain the significance of what is being portrayed. This task is left to the reader, who, entering into the mind of Joana, will interpret her words in a way that brings her to life as the protagonist of the novel. By focusing the reader's attention on Joana's inner turmoil, by alternating the temporal note, Clarice Lispector succeeded in making *Perto do coração selvagem* a novel that was as radically innovative in form as it was challenging in theme. Stunning in its effect on the Brazilian reading public in 1944, *selvagem* marked an auspicious debut for its nineteen-year-old author.

O lustre (1946)

More conventional in structure than *Perto do coração selvagem*, *O lustre* is also basically straightforward in its characterization. And like the previous work, *O lustre* develops around the gradually expanding awareness of its female protagonist, Virgínia, a woman whose gradual psychic alienation and destruction provide the thematic basis for the novel.

The central event in the development of Virgínia's early consciousness is her unexpected discovery of a drowned man in a river. Death and disintegration become, in fact, key forces in the novel. Daniel, Virgínia's brother, swears her to secrecy about the incident and she accedes to his demand. In the first half of the novel, Daniel exerts a powerful control over Virgínia and is largely responsible for what she says and does. Granja Quieta, where they live with the rest of their family, is a dark, densely described world that comes to have an oppressive atmosphere of its own. The normal routine of life in and around the family home is shattered when, again at the command of Daniel, Virgínia tells her father that Esmeralda, her sister, has been secretly meeting with a man in the garden behind the house. Surprisingly, the most important outcome of this deed is that Virgínia is forced to leave the family circle and make her way in the big city. Once Virgínia moves to the city, which is portrayed as having a fantastic, metallic, and anonymous presence, Daniel's role in the novel diminishes. As he ceases to be the decisive influence on Virgínia's identity, she is faced with a very human dilemma: whether to assume responsibility for her own existence or suffer the agony of knowing she has no sense of identity other than what other people choose to give her. Virgínia lives a solitary and grotesque life in the city, a life that the reader comes to know through a series of events that are simultaneously comic and pathetic in nature. Through it all, Virgínia is portrayed as being locked in a kind of social self-consciousness that prevents her from becoming anything more than an isolated observer of the events around her. Seeing the city through her eyes, the reader begins to realize how the sundry objects of its reality are being perceived by Virgínia's mind. Virgínia "grows" as a character, then, both in direct relation to her awareness of her own existence and as another object observed by other "objects," one rootlessly moving about an alien and sterile urban environment. In Virgínia's mind, inanimate objects slowly begin to acquire a luminous stability, while human beings are seen as undergoing a continuous and chaotic disintegration. Shards of their bodies, such as ears and fingernails, begin to obsess Virgínia, and she focuses more and more on them, thus never establishing a sense of wholeness about the people she meets.

Virgínia returns to her childhood home and the sharp but ironic differences between the country and the city are clearly shown. If the characters she encounters there possess tranquil existences, it is the tranquillity of solitude, isolation, and stagnation; and if the people of the city possess dynamism, it is the sterile, rootless, and pointless kind. A strong sense of contrast is also established between Virgínia's sense of her own childhood, representing a past now lost to her, and her present, which, though far from satisfactory, threatens to separate her ever farther from herself and from other beings.

Virgínia's response to this growing realization that existence for her is a lonely process of constantly becoming something else is to return to the city, where she feels her best chance for satisfaction lies. Taking a lover, Vicente, and subsequently discovering that for her love is now a conflict-ridden and paradoxical dead-end, Virgínia's life becomes a tragicomedy. She vacillates wildly between feelings of love and hate, aggression and timidity, humiliation and pride.

More and more she is undone by the virulence of her increasingly antithetical impulses; love, for example, seems a liberating force worth striving for yet it also appears to demand a kind of total submission to another being that she had experienced with her brother, Daniel. Hatred, on the other hand, is socially unacceptable yet capable of giving Virgínia a sense of power and strength she has never known.

Confused in her rational mind about who and what she is, Virgínia finally responds to a deeply felt impulse, the compulsion she feels to return again to the scene of her lost childhood and of the vision of death she had carried about in secret for so long. Later, returning to the city because she senses she cannot remain in Granja Quieta, that she is now a "different person," Virgínia is struck and killed by a car. Only as she is dying does Virgínia discover, ironically, the peace of mind she has sought so long.

The "action" of *O lustre* is as diffuse and psychological as it was in the first novel, *Perto do coração selvagem*. In both works, however, a woman's consciousness provides the filter through which the events of their lives are drawn. Both women realize that they are dissatisfied with their situations and both seek some way of improving them; Joana's attempt is acted out primarily in her mind, while Virgínia, more uncertain even than Joana, gravitates between two physical poles, the country and the city, in search of an authentic self. Both Joana and Virgínia attempt to establish their own identities by reacting to other people who are trying to influence them. Joana, for example, rejects the professor, Otávio, and Lídia in order to force herself to take responsibility for her own existence while Virgínia, in a less rational fashion, uses her relationship with Vicente to free herself first from Daniel's control and then from Vicente himself. As the reader sees in the conclusion of both novels, however, to win one's freedom does not, in Lispector's world, automatically guarantee happiness, satisfation, or fulfillment; indeed, the responsibility of being a free person may become virtually unbearable at times.

Like *Perto do coração selvagem*, *O lustre* is told primarily in the third person. But at certain key moments Lispector's third person transforms itself by entering into the mind of her protagonist. Whenever this shift in perspective occurs, the reader becomes aware of being privy to the inner thought processes of Virgínia herself. When Lispector wishes to establish an even stronger and more personal perspective for her protagonist, she has Virgínia express herself in the first person. The technical question of distance among the narrative voice, the minds of the protagonists, and the reader thus becomes as important an issue in *O lustre* as it was in the first novel.

Stylistically *O lustre* is considerably more poetic than *Perto do coração selvagem*. There is a metaphoric density and structural patterning in *O lustre* that exceeds Lispector's similar but more tentative efforts in the preceding work. The title of the work, *O lustre* ("the luster" or, in the context of the novel, "the chandelier"), itself signals one of the dominant images of the work. Like the lighthouse in Woolf's *To the Lighthouse,* the chandelier in the dining room of the *casarão* or country estate, functions as a structural motif that ties together the central themes and conflicts of the entire novel.

Developed through a prose permeated with the metaphoric interplay of light and dark (an interplay in which the chandelier has a key part) and references to "instants" of time and psychic recognition, *O lustre* is both more complex and more uneven than *Perto do coração selvagem*. But regardless of its shortcomings, *O lustre* was a bold stylistic step forward for Clarice Lispector and one that would carry her directly into her third novel.

A cidade sitiada (1949)

This novel, ironic in tone and considered by some to be Lispector's best, chronicles the past, present, and future of São Geraldo, a bustling suburb in the 1920s. The physical changes that are giving the town a new look and a new reality are absorbed into and refracted by the mind of the novel's protagonist, Lucrécia Neves.[2] Lucrécia, whose external or social life constantly contrasts with her inner or private life, is both drawn to and repelled by the city in which she lives. She marries Mateus, a foreign businessman who, in effect, promises her a newer, greater city, an offer she cannot resist. Once installed in the thoroughly bourgeois life of her new city, Lucrécia suddenly feels herself "out of place" and begins to experience a nostalgia for São Geraldo.

Metaphorically, Lucrécia Neves *is* the suburb, São Geraldo; the physical expansion of her town, in fact, parallels her own inner development as a person. Feeling increasingly estranged from her husband and from the big city, Lucrécia returns to São Geraldo. Noting the material growth of the suburb, she now feels pride for what she had once loathed. Having once spurned São Geraldo for the meretricious appeal of a newer, "better," more modern city, Lucrécia is suddenly transformed into a kind of booster for São Geraldo. But, her shallow materialism showing, Lucrécia soon grows complacent about the town, then becomes bored with it, and finally opts to leave it once again, enamored now of a new plan that she hopes will lead her on to new heights of "satisfaction."

A *cidade sitiada* resembles Lispector's earlier two novels in that it focuses on the way its protagonist absorbs, transforms, and finally personalizes the external world into patterns of imagery. It differs from *Perto do coração selvagem* and *O lustre,* however, in three major ways: A *cidade sitiada* is connected to a carefully described physical environment (São Geraldo) in a way the other two works were not; it is composed of scenes that are often comic in spirit (chapter 9, "O tesouro exposto" [The exposed treasure], sardonically depicts the sham and artificiality of middle-class marriage rites, for example); and, finally, A *cidade sitiada* employs a third-person narrative voice that does not, as in the other two novels, identify with the protagonist. Indeed, the narrative voice in A *cidade sitiada* actually deprecates and at times even satirizes Lucrécia herself, showing how the protagonist is not free of the very qualities, ideas, and habits that she disparages. In discovering the irony of this situation, the reader also comes to see an additional aspect of Lucrécia's personality, one that stands in stark contrast to anything possessed by either Joana or Virgínia—Lucrécia thinks in stereotypes. Without ever becoming aware of it (as Joana and Virgínia eventually do), Lucrécia is a prisoner of her cliché-ridden language, the expressive vehicle of her likewise cliché-ridden thought process.

In A *cidade sitiada* Clarice Lispector utilizes an interconnected pattern of images involving light, darkness, mirrors, water, and towers to translate the "reality" of São Geraldo into the ebb and flow that characterizes, albeit ironically, Lucrécia's mind. Lucrécia, however, is never fully aware of all that is happening around her or her role in it. She lacks the liberating strength, based for Clarice Lispector primarily on the fluctuations between states of love and hate, that wrenches Joana and Virgínia away from their petty, falsely based existences and leads them toward more authentic ones. This condition explains why status-conscious Lucrécia plays so many "roles" in the novel; she is alternately "idealistic" and materialistic, timid and aggressive, girl and woman, perfect (though stereotypical) wife and coquet. Lucrécia becomes, in short, whatever her external situation demands of her, a dimension of her physical and psychological environment.

Stylistically, *A cidade sitiada* is more like *Perto do coração selvagem* than *O lustre*. Lispector's third novel is simple and direct in its diction, although it is less densely metaphoric than *O lustre,* which is outstanding in this respect. But with its ironically developed process of characterization, the distance established between its narrative voice and its protagonist, and the importance it gives to specific external environment, *A cidade sitiada* signals some significant technical developments in Lispector's growth as a novelist.

A maçã no escuro (1961)

Lispector's fourth novel, *A maçã no escuro,* represents a turning point in her career. An allegory of the human condition[3] and lyrical in both structure and style, *A maçã no escuro* is the story of a man who struggles to create a new identity for himself. Just as he seems about to realize his goal, however, the man loses his courage and decides to reassume the comfortable though shallow and inauthentic identity he had originally possessed.

Martim, the protagonist of this dense, slow-moving novel, is a very ordinary person. He possesses no heroic proportions, yet his imperfectly understood compulsion to become a new person, to become more vitally tied to the most basic forces of existence, transforms his basically pathetic tale into an ironic quest. The object of his search, a goal that compels him but that he never really understands, is the attainment of what he feels must somehow be a mode of existence that is more personal and therefore more authentic than the social and superficial one he already has.

The reader meets Martim in medias res, as he is fleeing from a crime he thinks he has committed. In his muddled way, Martim interprets his crime, the attempted murder of his wife, as having been decisive for him in two ways: it represents the triumph of action over thought (which he feels has always rendered him incomplete and "inauthentic") and it has "liberated" him from his previous condition of passivity and acquiescence. He feels that his "liberating act," a crime against a person and a society, has shown him the way to a fuller realization of his true self, a part of his being that the constraints of society have blunted.

Martim's basic problem, however, is that he does not understand any of this very clearly. He wanders aimlessly through the darkness of a desert night and gradually begins to perceive himself somehow becoming a new person, of having experienced a kind of psychic rebirth. The first two basic divisions of the novel, "How a Man Is Made" and "The Birth of the Hero" (trans. Rabassa), help call the reader's attention to this process, one that becomes more complex as two equally unhappy and confused women, Vitória and Ermelinda, enter into Martim's inner struggle. The novel's third and final section, entitled "The Apple in the Dark," shows Martim on the verge of gaining at least a "new" life if not an "authentic existence," but lacking the resolution and determination necessary to render him a free person for very long. Ironically he allows himself to be meekly captured and led, a willing victim, back to society to do penance for his crime. The novel ends inconclusively, then, because the reader does not know what, if anything, Martim himself has learned from the entire affair.

The vagueness of the conclusion nonetheless turns out to be symptomatic of Lispector's primary theme. As is clear in her earlier three novels, Lispector's view of human relationships is a complex and not infrequently contradictory one. Martim, like Joana, was estranged from the people to whom, in a social (and therefore suspect) sense, he appeared closest; like Virgínia, he was aware of being manipulated by many of these same people, yet he became confused and insecure when their domination was removed. And like Lucrécia Neves, Martim was not committed to attaining real freedom; indeed, he was anxious to be led back into the protective, if perhaps emasculating, confines of society.

But for all the superficiality of Martim's psychic quest for a new sense of being, he showed himself to be an intensely human character. And in this sense his story has the ring of truth to it. As Martim attempted to strip away during his trek across the darkened desert the falseness and hypocrisy characteristic of much social behavior, he began to become aware of and then reject language, that most human and social of inventions. Reducing his sense of being to the level of rocks and stones, he proceeded to rebuild himself by rediscovering the primitive sources of language and trying to use it in more honest ways. Martim, like most of Lispector's characters, feels himself trapped in what critics like Jacques Derrida might call a prison of words, a web of self-referential intertextuality.

Martim's descent into the mysteries of his own being is thus undertaken with and charted by language, and this explains why language comes to play such a central role in the novel. Indeed, if one accepts the idea that our use of language determines what we think reality is, then language must be a crucial if not decisive aspect in the way we interpret our existence. Seen from this perspective *A maçã no escuro* concerns one man's understanding about who and what he is and about how he tries to use language to express what he discovers about himself. The "apple" of the title seems to symbolize the quest for knowledge,[4] mankind's desperate search for some solid, reassuring sense about the human condition, about our identity. The "darkness" that surrounds it, on the other hand, can be identified with the uncertainty, fear, and ignorance that make us doubt ourselves, that make us lose our courage and settle for being less than the free men and women we could be.

So although *A maçã no escuro* contains much that links it thematically to Lispector's first three novels, its closely woven structure, its systematically metaphorical rendering of a consciousness in flux, and, above all, its intense phenomenological preoccupation with language make it stand apart from the works that came before it. In signaling that a new plateau of artistic achievement had been reached by its author, *A maçã no escuro* anticipates the even more philosophical and lyrical novels that would follow.

A paixão segundo G. H. (1964)

One of the most singular Latin American novels of the 1960s, *A paixão segundo G. H.* tells the story of a woman who undergoes a mystical experience that changes the way she thinks about herself and about life. The protagonist, known to the reader by the initials G. H. embossed on a valise, premeditatedly crushes a cockroach in the door of a wardrobe. This apparently meaningless act suddenly reveals itself to the protagonist as having actually been the trigger that, once pulled, fires her into an inquisitional process of self-scrutiny and analysis. Overwhelmed by the rush of philosophical and personal implications that this act produces in her mind, G. H. is stripped of her quotidian sense of space and time and plunged into a maelstrom of ontological speculation about the nature of her being and about her place in the universe. As G. H. feels herself coming closer and closer to a personal understanding of the cosmos's most primitive and vital forces, she suddenly senses that by taking nourishment from the dead cockroach's body she can join these forces and thereby become one with the universe. In the novel's most powerful scene, G. H. experiences a kind of eucharist through the body of the crushed insect. Throughout, however, this act and the torrent of silent rumination that results from it are portrayed as being wholly sacred and never profane in nature. This treatment is consistent with Lispector's underlying theme that the urge to understand the truth about one's being and about one's place in the larger scheme of things is itself a wholly sacred issue, one not to be defiled by living "inauthentically."

The painful process by which G. H. comes to realize this great metaphysical truth is essentially that of the epiphany. The major structural difference is that Lispector succeeds in extending the moment of revelation to encompass about two-thirds of the novel. By eliminating dialogue and by divorcing the epiphanylike experience of G. H. from conventional time, Lispector is able to connect her protagonist's mystical experience with Begsonian "durée," the personal, nonchronological sense of inner time that the human mind can project over events.

As G. H.'s arcane experience begins to wane, the novel draws to a conclusion. At the end the reader sees G. H., fully aware of all that has happened to her and, more importantly, also aware of how she will attempt to put what she has learned into practice in her daily life. Reflecting on the meaning of what she has gone through, G. H. muses, "Eu, que havia vivido do meio do caminho, dera enfim o primeiro passo do seu começo"[5] (I who had always lived in the middle of the road, had finally taken the first step of its beginning). In a way that is analogous to Martim's self-liberating crime, G. H.'s experience with the cockroach "frees" her to enter into a higher level of understanding about herself. The primary difference between Martim and G. H. is that the latter is able not only to learn from her experience but also to live with her newly acquired knowledge as well.

Unlike the novels that came before it (including A maçã no escuro), A paixão segundo G. H. relies upon a self-reflective first-person narrator, one who is at the center of the action. But like the other novels, A paixão segundo G. H. centers on the still inner and overwhelmingly silent growth of a particular consciousness, one that is struggling, as all Lispector's protagonists do, to divine the meaning of the experience it is going through.[6] To the extent that language is treated both as the vehicle of communication and as an integral part of the quest for understanding itself, *A paixão segundo G. H.* is closely linked to *A maçã no escuro.* Structurally, *Perto do coração selvagem* has the advantage of being more concise than the sometimes diffuse *A maçã no escuro,* a work whose major flaw lies in its prolixity. The brevity of *A paixão segundo G. H.,* and the fact that it involves the drama of a single person, give it a structural unity and thematic intensity that make it one of Lispector's most accomplished novels.

Uma aprendizagem ou o livro dos prazeres (1969)

Uma aprendizagem ou o livro dos prazeres is a love story in the most complete sense of the term. A complex, multi-faceted novel, it is something of an anomaly as regards Lispector's other work, yet when read carefully it shows itself to be an elaboration of a theme that is endemic to Lispector's fiction: the nature of love and its function as a vital force in human affairs.

Uma aprendizagem has two major characters, a woman, Lóri, and a man, Ulisses. She is a schoolteacher who, feeling frustrated and socially constrained in Campos, the city in which she lives and works, journeys to Rio de Janeiro in search of personal freedom and a new life. Once there she meets Ulisses, a professor who is immediately attracted by Lóri's physical charms.

At first, as Ulisses begins to shower attention on Lóri, the reader feels that a rather routine seduction scenario is unfolding. But as Lóri and Ulisses talk (dialogue between the characters being one of the chief structural features that sets this novel apart from Lispector's other works), the reader learns that Ulisses has something else in mind and that he wants something more permanent and binding than a casual amorous encounter. Lóri, as seen through the language she uses, is portrayed as being adventurous and intelligent but, because of her family background and because she is a woman, also subject to manipulation by others, especially men. After dueling with Lóri over words and concepts, an activity that occupies the first third of the novel, Ulisses presents a long and seemingly sincere monologue on the nature of the human condition. The heart of this discourse involves the problematic ways love is understood and dealt with by men and women in twentieth-century society. As Ulisses puts it, "não temos usado a palavra amor para não termos de reconhecer sua contextura de ódio, de amor, de ciúme e de tantos outros contraditórios"[7] (we haven't used the word "love" so as not to have to recognize its contextuality of hate, of love, of jealousy and so many other contradictions). He goes on to say that to speak of what "really matters" is considered a social gaffe and that men and women fear themselves and what they feel as well as each other. But, Ulisses says in conclusion, he has finally escaped all this; he will wait for Lóri until she, too, can free herself, as he believes he has freed himself, from all that prevents her from becoming her own person. Lóri, who has had a string of unsuccessful love affairs, is touched but perplexed by this declaration of love and freedom by Ulisses.

Time passes and Lóri and Ulisses come to know more and more about each other until finally Lóri, who does grow in strength and freedom, predicts that one day Ulisses's "impersonality" will join with her "individuality" and they will become one. Although Lóri and Ulisses accept the idea that they will ultimately become lovers, they both sense that somehow the time is not yet right, that their relationship is still not based on what it should be based; some vital element, one not yet clearly understood, is missing. The conclusion of the novel is given over to their discovery of this "missing element," the one that makes their love both authentic and enduring.

This missing key ingredient, Lóri and Ulisses discover, is the kind of freedom that comes from total and complete psychological independence. Their dialogues suggest that only by possessing the strength demanded of truly free people can we give ourselves over to the unconditional but mutual surrender that is love. Only if they first attain states of authentic individual freedom can Lóri and Ulisses hope to attain the state of total, loving submission that they desire. Or, as Lóri and Ulisses demonstrate, the surrender of love can occur only if each part is free to begin with. Realizing that true, self-affirming, self-fulfilling love cannot take place until both parties are free to choose, Lóri and Ulisses part company rather than accept something "inauthentic."

Lóri, owing to her position as a woman in Brazilian (one may read "world") society, has further to come in this regard than does Ulisses, who only has to understand the potentially lethal attractions of power and the importance of what some critics have termed "sexual politics." Near the end of the novel, Lóri experiences late one rainy night her moment of revelation, her liberating epiphany.

Suddenly assuming full responsibility for who and what she is, Lóri freely and fearlessly chooses to give herself, body and soul, to Ulisses, who responds to her in like manner. Invincible not in their union as lovers but in their union as free, aware human beings who, being individuals, have chosen to unite as lovers, Lóri and Ulisses make love and lay plans for the complexities and challenges of a lifetime spent together.

Uma aprendizagem ou o livro dos prazeres is different in several respects from Lispector's other novels: it relies heavily on dialogue (and not monologue) to achieve its desired characterizations;[8] the dialogues themselves show how two people were able to succeed in drawing closer to each other (previously Lispector had used dialogue chiefly to show how interpersonal communication fails); and, in asserting the potentially self-affirming strength of love (though never forgetting that, if mishandled, love becomes a cruelly divisive force), *Uma aprendizagem* emerges as Lispector's most positive and optimistic tale.

But there are other differences as well, differences that point to a Lispector of greater range and technical diversity than had been previously seen. There are two major characters rather than one, and although they both seek the venerable Lispectorian goal of self-realization and authenticity of being, they seek it for themselves, ironically, by giving themselves away in love. Lóri, moreover, brings a healthy, animal-like sexuality to Ulisses, who had been lacking this kind of carnal vitality, and he in turn shows her the way to personal freedom. This is the "apprenticeship" referred to in the title; we should use the act of living to find freedom and love for ourselves and then to help others find the same things.

The most notable feature of this novel, however, may be its social relevancy. Few topics are more "socially relevant" than the issue of how men and women relate to each other, and, as we see in the story of Lóri and Ulisses, this is the core that Lispector builds her story around. When, late in the novel, the newly free and newly whole Lóri wonders if her "enormous liberty" (173) will "offend" people of her social strata, Ulisses, speaking for the male-dominated majority (which includes both men and women), says, yes, of course it will: "Porque você acaba de sair da prisão como ser livre, e isso ninguém perdoa. O sexo e o amor não te são proibidos. Você enfim aprendeu a existir. E isso provoca o desencadeamento de muitas outras liberdades, o que é risco para a tua sociedade" (173: Because you've just left prison as a free person, and nobody pardons this. Sex and love are no longer prohibited for you. You've finally learned to exist. And this will set off a chain reaction of other liberties, all of which are a risk for your society).

Lispector's sixth novel stands out, then, for its use of constructive, positive dialogue rather than anguished, disconnected inner monologue, for its use of two focal-point characters whose combined, mutually sustaining experience give humankind at least hope, and for its presentation of love as the only human force capable of breaking down the walls of isolation that our language and our physical existence seem to build around us. But while all these features do indeed characterize it, *Uma aprendizagem* is perhaps most memorable for its overall value as a social statement about how honest, sincere, and, above all, free men and women might learn to care better for each other. Were this to occur, the "apprenticeship" that is human life would result in a society more beneficial to all, one based on freedom, love, and equality.

Água viva (1973)

Água viva, Lispector's seventh novel (she herself called it a "fiction"), exceeds even *A maçã no escuro* in the refined lyricism of its style and structuring. Although *Água viva* concerns the psychological struggle of a woman to grow by freeing herself from a restricting love affair, the creation of the text itself is what the novel is really about. Continuously transforming events and ideas into the sensations they elicit in the mind of the female protagonist, *Água viva* is close to being a prose poem in its metaphoric expressiveness. As pure and successful an example of the lyrical novel form as Lispector ever wrote, *Água viva* still retains the narrative sinew of a story that is being told to someone else, however.

Adopting a form that is confessional or diarylike in its intimacy and precision, *Água viva* traces the quest of its unnamed and virtually undescribed protagonist for a state of psychological freedom. In this respect clearly related to its predecessor, *Uma aprendizagem ou o livro dos prazeres, Água viva* is, however, once again deeply personal rather than socially relevant in its themes.

When the reader first meets her, the protagonist is in the process of writing a letter to an unnamed lover. Gradually the reader learns that although the "I" who is "talking" and thinking—who is in effect telling the story—wants to terminate a relationship, she (we know it is a woman because of certain grammatical features) wants to do so in a way that will "free" her ex-lover as well. Following the thematic treatment of love described in *Uma aprendizagem,* the narrator of *Água viva* realizes that the relationship she currently has cannot develop any further. It cannot yield any more satisfaction because the parties involved are not both strong and free individuals; the narrator is, but her lover is not, and their relationship cannot, therefore, succeed. She realizes, too, that there is a limit to how much she can help the other person. She can tell him what he has to do to free himself, how he must change, but in the end it is up to him and no one else to do so. Anticipating her lover's refusal to try or his likely failure to succeed in becoming a free person, the narrator in *Água viva* is preparing to continue growing herself, to experience, through another act of liberation (her decision to leave a dying relationship), a new "rebirth," a new life. She writes, near the end of the novel, "Fui ao encontro de mim. . . . Simplesmente eu sou eu. E você é você. . . . Olha para mim e me ama, Não: tu olhas para ti e te amas"[9] (I went to an encounter with myself. . . . I am simply me. And you are you. . . . Look at me and love me, No: you look at yourself and love yourself).

Structurally *Água viva* consists of an unbroken monologue. The psychological depth of this monologue, which takes the form of a letter, varies in accordance with the degree to which the subject matter dealt with at each point stimulates a response in the mind of the narrator, the person writing the letter. Thus, as the narrator dicusses the need for an honest and free existence, she becomes personally swept up in her own epiphanylike revelations. Her overpowering sense of "rebirth," of renewal, is conveyed to the reader through patterns of interlocking images and metaphors. All of Lispector's characteristic motifs are utilized: images of light and darkness, the symbolism of water and birth, the mystical awareness that comes through silence, the structuring of one's inner existence through a concatenation of "now-instants" and, finally, concern over the mysterious power of words.

As the narrator operates on the upper level of her conscious mind, the letter she writes seems to be the very text we read, that is, the novel *Água viva* itself. But whenever her sentient, truth-seeking mind is set off by a thought, the text is suddenly transformed from an explanatory discourse into a hermetic but visually powerful poem.

When this occurs, the images that come into play represent the ideas that lie behind the words, the skein of thoughts that remain locked in their silence behind the word-object, the thing made of breath or ink that we create, the virtually tactile thing that symbolizes the intangibilities of what we think and feel. This ontological concern over language, reality, and the human capacity to express it, to "communicate" thoughts about reality, has been a benchmark of Lispector's fiction ever since *Perto do coração selvagem* and it continues here. As Lispector's most successful lyrical novel, *Água viva* achieves a powerful and affective union of these pronounced philosophic and linguistic concerns. Brought to life through a style that is "realistic" in its ability to name and describe in detail specific things in the three-dimensional world but to do so via a style that is also "poetic" in its ability to express imagistically the psychic reactions these concrete things produce in the mind of a protagonist, *Água viva* represents a triumph of control, selectivity, and focus on Lispector's part. Just as *A paixão segundo G. H.* must be considered one of the most powerful Latin American novels of the 1960s, so, too, must *Água viva* rank as one of the outstanding achievements of the 1970s.

In *Água viva,* one of Lispector's most intense efforts, the central image is water. In a sense, water, in its several forms (one of the major ones involves birth), serves as a metaphor for the text's very structuring, which is fluid and free-flowing. Images involving water not only dot the narrative but equate its thematic concerns, chiefly concerned with the gradual self-realization of the narrative voice, with life, fertility and, above all, birth. This use of water imagery to reflect a growing self-awareness on the part of her female protagonists is common in Lispector's work and can be traced back to Joana's experience with the ocean and her bath in *Perto do coração selvagem*.

At the center of the narrative, and holding it together, is the self-conscious, first-person voice that tells the story. There are two sources of conflict for the woman whose point of view in the novel emerges and develops as a long indirect interior monologue. Read as a letter that is designed to break off an unsatisfactory love affair, *Água viva*'s initial protagonal conflict is basically interpersonal in nature. Within this socially oriented conflict, however, is another one, an ontological conflict that rests on the protagonist's acutely private and lonely struggle to free herself from false modes of being, to grasp the truth of the human condition and to make this truth her own. Reflecting the primitivism that is endemic to Lispector's work, the narrator/protagonist of *Água viva* tells us what she is seeking: "I want the plasma, I want to feed directly from the placenta. . . . I'm trying to capture the fourth dimension of the now-instant, which, so fleeting, is no longer" (9).

Like Lispector herself (who never exhibited her paintings), the narrator of *Água viva* is a painter who also writes. Thus the aesthetic issue of how best to express one's inner reality—through painting or through language—enters into the text of *Água viva* itself, which, we know, is primarily concerned with the narrator's attempt to free herself from entanglements that are both external (her failing and therefore potentially ruinous love affair) and internal (her own timidity). She writes:

I want to capture my *is*. . . . I write to you feeling whole, with a zest for life. . . . I paint my pictures with my whole body and I affix the corporeal to the canvas. . . . When you read me you will ask why I do not restrict myself to painting . . . since I write roughly and without order. The answer is that now I feel the need for words, and what I write is new for me because my true word was, until now, untouched. The word is my fourth dimension. (10)

The poetic, steadily metaphoric structuring of *Água viva* reflects the growth and final "birth" (or "rebirth") of the narrator's consciousness. This is what the text "is about." Within the confines of the lyrical novel genre, one can trace in *Água viva* the development of the narrative's focal point "I," its organizing perspective. The tension and intensity generated by *Água viva* are entirely mental in nature, however, for, typical of the lyrical novel, little in the way of physical action comes into play. The narrator's psychic condition is far from static, however; indeed, it ebbs and flows, like water, in constant motion but not always with a sure sense of progress. In order to trace the narrator's inner divagations, which only circuitously lead toward a final self-affirming state of freedom, the reader must read slowly and carefully, savoring each word of the narrator's silent monologue as one would the words of a lyric poem. We read:

My effort: to bring the future to the present. I move within my deep
instincts, which fulfill themselves blindly. I feel close to fountains, lakes
and waterfalls, all overflowing with abundant waters. And I am free. (30)

Then, in a state of reverie, she declares, "My eyes are closed . . .
I'm pure unconsciousness. They have already cut the umbilical
cord. . . . I'm loose in the universe" (38). Sensing the "rebirth"
that, for her, may be imminent, the voice says, "I am making
myself. . . . I make myself until I reach the core. . . . Now, at
dawn, I am pale and panting and my mouth is dry in the face of
what I achieve" (41).

The narrator, struggling and ultimately achieving her own self-
affirming freedom, realizes, though, that "I don't yet know where
my freedom will take me" (33). Then, in an act that recalls the
treatment of love in *Uma aprendizagem ou o livro dos prazeres,* the
protagonist of *Água viva,* newly liberated (internally and externally)
freely bestows a similar state of freedom on her ex-lover: "I'm giving
you freedom . . . before I break the water sack. Then I shall cut
the umbilical cord . . . and you will be alive, on your own" (35).
Suggesting here, in an ironic way, that authentic freedom, which
demands a special honesty and strength and which also imposes a
special kind of solitude on a person, is not as desirable as is commonly
thought, the narrator proves her own courage, independence, and
resolve by forging ahead, by assuming responsibility for the authenticity of her existence. Yet she does not attain it at the expense
of someone else. Ironically, the narrator does not so much grant her
former lover's freedom as she imposes it on him, demanding, as it
were, that he either assume it in all of its dimensions or that he
retreat into false modes of existence. This poetic yet sharply philosophic monologue continues to the end of the novel, which comes
to a halt with typical Lispectorian ambiguity: "I am simply myself.
And you are you. It's vast, it will last. What I write is a *this.* It
won't stop, it will continue. . . . What I write you continues,
and I am simply bewitched" (97).

With this uncertain, ambiguous conclusion, which ambivalently
suggests both the process of becoming (a primary thematic motif
of Lispector's work) and the culmination of this process for the
protagonist, *Água viva* underscores its own structural fluidity. Embodying the kind of verisimilitude (of discourse and of silence) that
Tzvetan Todorov speaks of in *The Poetics of Prose,*[10] the "voice" of

Água viva establishes her own, deeply private reality by means of language; put another way, the narrator, through the actual writing of her letter (the text we read) and through her silent battle to understand the concepts she sought to control through words, creates herself, her own truth, her own verisimilitude. Her "reality," as a character, therefore, must be evaluated not in terms of action or external events but in terms of her struggle to comprehend the mutable, imbalanced growth of her self-consciousness. There exists, surprisingly, a certain kind of plot structure in *Água viva,* one that can be traced through the slow evolution of the narrator's self-awareness and sense of personal freedom.

The narrator's conflict, as we have seen, is profoundly personal and only imperfectly perceived by her; indeed, the narrative itself not only reflects but actually is (since the narrative voice is simultaneously writing and thinking out the very words that give form to the text we read) the working out of this key conflict, the narrator's realization of self, of a newly independent and authentic identity. And, as in virtually all of Lispector's fiction, language (always used in relation to the realities it is said to describe and the idiosyncrasies of the mind that uses it to identify things) is both the subject matter of the work and the means by which that subject matter is examined. Seen in this light, *Água viva* shows itself to be a refinement of the phenomenological interrelations among language, identity, and reality, this being an issue that, for Lispector, first surfaced in a coordinated fashion in *A maçã no escuro.* These two works, *A maçã no escuro* and the more distilled *Água viva,* go further than any of Lispector's other similarly phenomenological works in showing how her fiction is fully representative of what critics like Georges Poulet ("Phenomenology of Reading"), Roman Ingarden (*The Cognition of the Literary Work of Art,* 1973), Julia Kristeva (*Desire in Language,* 1980), Hans-Georg Gadamer (*Truth and Method,* 1975), Wolfgang Iser (*The Implied Reader,* 1974), Hans Robert Jauss (his theory concerning the aesthetics of reception), Roland Barthes (*The Pleasure of the Text,* 1976), or Jacques Derrida (*Of Grammatology,* 1976) were stressing in regard to the crucial role language plays in human existence, literature, and in our response to it. Always concerned with getting at the truth of things, with interpreting the ephemeral relationships between language and reality, and the human perception of both, Clarice Lispector was an author whose work lends itself to the kind of critical approaches advocated by these and other post-World War II critics. Much more can and should be done in this regard to Lispector's fiction, and of all her novels and stories *Água viva* would be an ideal starting point.

Conveying the flux of the narrator's several levels of self-awareness, the patterns of imagery in *Água viva* mark her retrograde progress toward her still fluid but increasingly confident condition at the end of the book. As we read:

I enter slowly into my gift to myself, a splendor dilacerated by the last song which seems to be the first. I enter slowly into writing just as I entered into painting. It is a tangled world of liana vines, syllables, honeysuckles, colors and words—the threshold of the ancestral cavern which is the uterus of the world, and out of it I shall be born. (15)

Using words metaphorically and not denotatively, as if to paint her violently evolving inner vision of self, the narrative voice grows ever more conscious of her own emergent identity:

My hand rests upon the earth and listens, hotly, to the beating of a heart. I see a large white slug with a woman's breasts . . . is it a human being? I burn it in an inquisitional fire. I possess the mysticism of shadows from a remote past. . . . Elementary creatures surround me, dwarfs, goblins, gnomes and genies. I sacrifice animals to take from them the blood I need for my occult ceremonies. In my fury I offer my soul in its own blackness. (39)

Fully self-conscious not only of her own, inner tumult but of her external role as author, as the rational controller of the chaotically imagistic text she is creating, the narrator declares:

I breathe energy at night. And all this so fantastic . . . fantastic . . . for one instant the world is exactly what my heart demands. I'm ready to die and form new compositions. I'm expressing myself very badly and the right words escape me. My internal form is finely distilled and yet my connection with the world has the naked crudity of free dreams and great realities. . . . (41)

But because the structure of *Água viva* is integrally bound up in the narrative voice's metaphoric and speculative quest for a more authentic identity and self-consciousness, the text itself draws to a close (as opposed to a conflict resolving conclusion) that finds its parallel in the narrator's increasing satisfaction with what she has achieved (freed herself and her erstwhile lover) and with what she will become in the future (an even stronger and more aware human being). Beginning finally to realize the destruction (of the fearful and inauthentic realities, often other people, that surround and touch her life) that can result from our efforts to free ourselves, the narrator notes, not without pain:

I sense we will soon separate. My astonishing truth is that I was always yours alone and I didn't know it. Now I know. Now I am alone, with myself and my bewildering freedom . . . the huge responsibility of solitude. (73)

Resolving, finally, to do the best she can with her newly won freedom, but also trying to damage as little as possible her former lover (whom we suspect will not be able to free himself from his false identity), the narrator plans her strategy, the one that will bring her letter, her self-affirming discourse, to a close:

This afternoon we will see each other. And I won't say a word about what I'm writing to you, what contains what I am, and what I give you as a gift, even though you don't read it. And when I've written down the secret of my being, I'll throw it away, like a bottle into the sea. I write to you because you do not accept what I am. When I destroy my notations of the instants, will I return to the nothingness from where I took everything? I have to pay the price, the price of someone with a past who renews himself with passion in the strange present. When I think of what I've already lived it seems I've left bodies strewn along the way. . . . I block the pain of what I write to you and I offer you my restless happiness. (74–75)

Composed of "now-instants" and revelations, *Água viva,* a text based on a "personal experience"[11] of Lispector's, is a narrative that works on the reader like a poem. Political in that it is based thematically on the assumption that healthy human relationships must be built carefully on the twin pillars of love and freedom, *Água viva* nevertheless comes alive through its language, a supple vehicle of expression for Clarice Lispector and one that relies heavily on the mechanics and functions of poetry to reach the deepest parts of our vital human concerns over the nature of being and identity. *Água viva* is a powerful, affective novel, one that is in the critical and

philosophic mainstream of Western literature in the second half of
the twentieth century.

A hora da estrela (1977)

Lispector's penultimate novel, one much praised by many critics,
and the last of her novels to be published before her death later in
1977, *A hora da estrela* represents a departure from the intensely
lyrical structuring of *Água viva*. Responding, perhaps, to a personal
need to make her highly subjective fiction more expressive of certain
sociopolitical themes of urgent importance for Brazil, Lispector wrote
in *A hora da estrela* a novel that attempts to merge the lyricism and
hermeticism so characteristic of her best work with a theme of overt
"social relevancy." The theme in question, one that contained autobiographical implications for Lispector, has to do with the ways
Brazil's poverty-ridden Northeast blunts the lives of the people who
live there, crippling them in ways that almost inevitably condemn
them to unhappiness and frustration.

Specifically, *A hora da estrela* relates the pathetic story of Macabéa,
a young *nordestina* (a woman from the Northeast) who, representing
a real sociological phenomenon, emigrates to the cities of the industrial South in search of a better life.

Macabéa is a unique kind of protagonist for Clarice Lispector;
because of the thinness of her basic education and because of the
generally blighted social milieu in which she was reared, Macabéa
does not possess the psychological strength and intellectual daring
of such characters as Joana, G. H., or even Lóri. Macabéa is actually
more like a materially poor and less self-conscious version of Lucrécia
Neves than she is like most of Lispector's other protagonists. Even
the "better life" that Macabéa seeks (like Martim, in a very confused
way) is predicated on a vague idea she has about the superiority of
material things over nonmaterial things.

The problem Lispector faced in developing Macabéa was basically
the same one Graciliano Ramos faced with Fabiano and Vitória in
Vidas sêcas (1938), a novel that Lispector must certainly have known.
The problem, essentially, is this: how does a writer develop a character who, like Macabéa, Fabiano, and Vitória, does not possess
much formal education, does not handle language well, and who is
largely oblivious to the intellectual concepts language purports to
express? Both Lispector and Ramos deal with this issue by relying

on indirect discourse and on similes, metaphors, and scenes that show the reader what the characters are like. Lispector, however, perhaps because she was less comfortable than Ramos in using backlands imagery, is not always successful in depicting Macabéa's character in this fashion. The result is that Macabéa is one of Lispector's less convincing, less moving characters although she does command an undeniable symbolic significance, that of the psychological effects of poverty on a human being.

Lispector is much more successful in showing the reader what befalls Macabéa in the strange and hostile urban environment into which she, refugeelike, is thrown. Possessed of an innocence and naiveté that is at once comical and pathetic, Macabéa quickly falls under the influence of Olímpico, who is also a refugee from the Northeast. As a character Olímpico reflects the psychological trappings of a male-dominated culture and shows himself to be both bombastic and ludicrous in his "relationship" with Macabéa. He, too, is a victim, though as long as he has Macabéa he has someone to whom he can continue to play the role of a kind of deluded "master." The sad "master/slave" relationship that develops (each of them merely playing out their stereotypical roles) between Macabéa and Olímpico reflects the two fundamental aspects of Lispector's social consciousness: her concern over the ways men and women deal with each other (to judge by the standards established in *Uma aprendizagem*, there is little chance here for an authentic love relationship to develop) and her awareness of the Northeast as representing a very severe human problem for Brazilian society in general. Surprisingly, this places Lispector in a long tradition of Brazilian writers, one headed by Euclides da Cunha and his epic *Os sertões* (1902; trans. Putnam, *Rebellion in the Backlands*).

Technically *A hora da estrela* is different from Lispector's other works because it employs a wholly self-conscious narrator, one Rodrigo S. M., a man who is fully conscious of writing a text in which there are characters he creates and with whom he is involved. One of these characters, Macabéa, will so powerfully affect the narrator's sensibilities that when she "dies" he "dies" as well.[12] The basic structural irony of the text stems from the narrator's self-conscious deliberation about his role in the novel and what he should have happen to Macabéa. After Macabéa is struck by a car—a yellow Mercedes—and killed, he says of her, "Eu poderia deixá-la na rua e simplesmente não acabar a história. Mas não . . ."[13] (I could simply leave her there in the street and simply not finish the story. But I won't . . .). Lispector's narrator weaves in and out of his own narrative, now speaking in his own voice about the problems of writing such a novel, now describing the action in novelistically orthodox ways. The result is a symbolic work that, ironic in its self-conscious structural complexity, is an interesting if not completely successful attempt to put Lispector's sensitivity to the inner realm at the service of a major social problem. As such, it makes one wonder what kind of novels and stories would have followed it had its author not died in the year of its publication.

Um sopro de vida (1978)

Begun in 1974 but not completed until 1977, just before its author's death, Um sopro de vida was published posthumously in 1978. Written concurrently with A hora da estrela, the manuscripts of Um sopro de vida were ordered, arranged, and finally published in book form by Lispector's friend and confidante, Olga Borelli.

Dealing, as it does, with a soul baring itself in the face of an anticipated death, Um sopro de vida is a painful if loving book. More a confession than a novel,[14] and full of facts and references that are frequently as autobiographical as they are fictional, Um sopro de vida develops as a long, lyrical poem rather than as even a lyrical novel.

Divided into four sections, "Um sopro de vida" (A breath of life), "O sonho acordado é que é a realidade" (Reality is a waking dream), "Como tornar tudo um sonho acordado?" (How can everything become a waking dream?), and "Livro de Ângela" (The book of Ângela), Um sopro de vida is written in a self-conscious first-person mode: "Este livro é a sombra de mim . . ."[15] (This book is my shadow . . .); "Eu não faço literatura: eu apenas vivo ao correr do tempo. O resultado fatal de eu viver é o ato de escrever" (15: I'm not writing literature; I'm only living in the flow of time. The fatal result of my living is the act of writing).

The narrative voice, seemingly that of Lispector herself, comes to feel the need for another presence in the text, someone to talk to, to communicate with. The result is the narrator's creation of Ângela Pralini, a name that also belongs to a character who played a major role in one of Lispector's earlier stories, "Felicidade clandestina" (from Felicidade Clandestina).

Just as God breathed life into Man, so, too, does our narrator "breathe life" ("um sopro de vida") into Angela, a character who then begins a colloquy with the narrator and permits the narrator to use her as a foil for a heightened and more telling self-scrutiny. At this point in the narrative, the term *sopro* ("breath") assumes a dual role; it becomes a metaphor for the act of creation, literary and otherwise, but it also expands into a larger and more comprehensive metaphor for life itself *(vida)*, for the vital and aware act of living.

As in *A hora da estrela,* *Um sopro de vida* labors to establish a link between art and society and between the day-to-day realities of men and women. And while both works make use of a self-conscious narrator to develop this theme, *Um sopro de vida* carries it further and personalizes it at least insofar as we come to feel, at the conclusion, that the narrator/author is really Lispector herself. The penultimate line of the novel, which is enclosed in quotation marks, seems to suggest that it is Lispector herself who enters the text here, the text that is being created by her narrator and her narrator's own creation, Ângela Pralini. Interpreting the line in this fashion, Lispector's own voice would provide a final and perhaps desperate comment on the idea broached a few pages before about how the artist avoids the oblivion of death by living forever through his art. Mysteriously punctuated and uncertain as to its speaker, this key penultimate line reads, "Eu . . . eu . . . não. Não posso acabar" (162: I . . . I . . . no. I can't come to an end).

Structurally uneven and sometimes overly abrupt in its transitions (owing probably to the circumstances surrounding its final composition), *Um sopro de vida* nevertheless exerts a powerful hold on the reader. Intensely musical and more a poem than a narrative, *Um sopro de vida* is confessional in both theme and form. Its irony, however, as in *A hora da estrela,* stems from the pose struck by its narrative voice and reminds one of Byron's *Don Juan* in its self-conscious awareness of "not knowing" how best to proceed.

Though not widely recognized as an ironic writer, Clarice Lispector was quite aware of how irony could play an important role in her work. The multiple ironies involving Lucrécia Neves, for example, in *A cidade sitiada* prove that even early on Lispector was quite capable of letting irony play a significant role in the characterizations of her typically introspective and self-aware protagonists. And while irony is decisively present in the case of Lucrécia Neves, it is also present in *A maçã no escuro* and in the final section of *Perto do coração selvagem,* when the possibly naive Joana is bravely making plans to do battle with a world the hypocrisy and treachery of which she is poorly equipped to comprehend. The reader suspects what Joana herself does not seem to consider, that she is going into this battle unarmed, or that she is bearing the wrong kind of weapon. Still, the novel focuses on her earlier personal revelation and not what she will or will not make of it.

But in *Um sopro de vida* this is not the case; the reader is closely drawn to the narrator/author, Clarice Lispector or not, and feels, either way, that this person—this human being—has fought the battle of life the way we would all like to fight it—with courage, sincerity, and dignity. As the text develops, the narrator/author openly seeks the reader's confidence and shows him that the final solution of the problem posed by the narrative is unclear even to the person telling the story. As in Byron's *Don Juan,* the structural pose demanded by the presence of "romantic irony" allows Clarice Lispector to continue to the end her self-doubting quest for truth and understanding at the same time that it allows her to develop the focal-point character, the character who is able to lure the reader into his or her inner world. The reader identifies more personally and in a less abstract way with the central consciousness in *Um sopro de vida* because the basic issue, how one handles the knowledge of one's impending death, is presented in a deeply personal and confessional mode; through its style and structure, the problem confronted in *Um sopro de vida* is made to seem the reader's problem as much as the protagonist's.

Because of the extreme nature of the circumstances surrounding its creation, *Um sopro de vida* cannot be judged on quite the same critical grounds as Lispector's other novels. Thematically, however, "a breath of life" is what the characters of Clarice Lispector have always sought. And so, with their creator here entering the fray with them, *Um sopro de vida* can be read as Lispector's final statement about the meaning of life and the value of art in it.

• • •

As is true of her novels, Lispector's stories (especially her early ones) are basically structured on moments of inner vision or awareness. The primary difference is that in the stories there is usually only one moment of insight or vision while in the longer form of the novel there are several of these moments. The novels, in fact, are actually concatenations of epiphanies, and although they take on a pattern or design that we associate with the lyrical novel, they give up the sense of action and event that we associate with realistic fiction. Lispector's short fiction, which many critics consider her real brilliance as a writer, has an economy of expression, intensity, and a sharpness of focus that the more diffuse, more fluid novels do not possess.

In a large part, this intensity and focus derive from the nature of the modern story form itself. Structured more around the exposition of a character's nature through a single event (rather than on the slow, novelistic exposition of a character's personality), the story medium is well suited to Lispector's thematic and stylistic interests. These interests, always rooted in Lispector's fascination with language and with the mystery and power of the human mind, help show how much her stories have in common with Joyce's stories, especially those of *Dubliners* (1916), the collection of short pieces that first began to illustrate how Joyce was going to revolutionize the modern short-story form by placing a religious term, the epiphany, at the service of fiction.[16]

Alguns contos (1952)

Published in 1952, three years after her third novel (and six years after Rosa's *Sagarana*), *Alguns contos* was Lispector's first collection of stories. Immediately praised by the critics, the six short stories that make up the collection, "Mistério em São Cristóvão" ("Mystery in São Cristóvão"), "Os laços de família" ("Family Ties"), "Começos de uma fortuna" ("The Beginnings of a Fortune"), "Amor" ("Love"), "Uma galinha" ("A Chicken"), and "O jantar" ("The Dinner"), would later be included in the collection entitled *Laços de família* (1960).

Just as Lispector's novels had helped change the course of development for the Brazilian novel, so, too, did the short fiction of *Alguns contos* alter the way the Brazilian short story would be written. As with her novels, Lispector's stories focused not on the external world of action and event but on the inner world of psychological drama and conflict.

Written in a lyrical mode with a language heavily charged with ambiguity, metaphor, and nuance, the stories of *Alguns contos* are also structured around the concept of the epiphany. Thus a tale like the atmospheric yet powerful "Love" is not so much about something that happens as much as it is about the way Ana (Anna in Pontiero's translation), the main character, perceives and responds to what happens around her. Nothing really happens to Ana; she is a content, complacent middle-class wife and mother whose life is based on her notions of order, control, and the stability of things. Having boarded a tram and heading home after a shopping trip, Ana's secure world is unexpectedly shattered as she suddenly sees a blind man chewing gum. With the point of view taking the reader inside Ana's now reeling mind, we learn, "Um cego mascando chicles mergulhara o mundo em escura sofreguidão"[17] (A blind man chewing gum has plunged the world into a mysterious excitement).

Completely disoriented by this experience, Ana stumbles off the tram at the wrong stop. Finding herself in the Botanical Gardens, she senses a primitive, threatening world all about her. Wandering through it, lost in a hostile but primary environment, Ana's mind is stripped of its false convictions, and she comes into contact with the most basic and elemental aspects of her being. We read, "O Jardim Botânico, tranqüilo e alto, lhe revelava. Com horror descobria que pertencia à parte forte do mundo . . ." (38: The Botanical Garden, tranquil and high, had been a revelation. With horror, she discovered that she belonged to the strong part of the world . . .).

Later, when she had made her way home and her world had returned to normal, Ana wonders to herself if her experience will "fill her days" or if, in her domestic tranquillity, she will be removed from the "danger of living" represented by her momentary closeness to the "savage heart of life."

Prototypical as it is of Lispector's short fiction, "Amor" ("Love") deserves special critical attention. All of the elements characteristic of Lispector's work can be found in this story, which is perhaps her best known and most anthologized piece of writing. As we have seen, the tale involves a woman's totally unsettling inner experience, one that heightens her awareness of who and what she is and one that forces her to choose, at the conclusion of the story, what kind of life she will lead thereafter. In addition to this, however, a delicate ambiguity permeates the woman's final decision and thus establishes a note of tension where we would normally expect a resolution of the basic conflict.

Although the style of "Love" is metaphoric and referentially oblique ("On the ground there lay dry fruit stones of circumvolutions like small rotted cerebrums"[18] and "Anna took the moment like a butterfly, between her fingers before it might escape forever" [47]) the story reveals itself best through an analysis of Anna's character and of its structure.

When the reader first meets her, Anna, the protagonist, is portrayed as the epitome of the middle-class wife and mother, a woman whose entire sense of being rests solely on her rigorously conventional domestic and social status. Coming home on a streetcar from a shopping trip, Anna sighs with "satisfaction" as she reflects "with certainty and pleasure" about her "nice" children and her dependable, predictable husband, about whom we learn virtually nothing in the story (37–38). The reader gradually comes to realize, however, that although Anna "seemed to have discovered that everything was capable of being perfected, that each thing could be given a harmonious appearance," that "life itself could be created by Man" (38), she was still disturbed by something, something that was intangible but which she feared. Anna, the chief organizer of a shallow, materialistic world based more on appearances than essences, on a false sense of "control," became "anxious" when "nothing more required her strengths." Ironically, the narrative voice informs the reader that "deep down, Anna had always found it necessary to feel the firm root of things. And this is what a home had surprisingly provided" (38). The irony of this description of Anna becomes apparent only after reading the rest of the story and seeing how far, in fact, Anna's sense of security and identity (both based falsely on her bourgeois existence) was from "the firm root of things." So while Lispector wastes no time in establishing Anna's basic character (and thereby stressing the flaw in it, that is, its Sartrean "inauthenticity"), she also prepares the reader for the upcoming conflict by suggesting that when Anna could not "control" things, she became "anxious."

As the details of Anna's superficial and basically fearful existence grow in number, thus concretizing Anna as a character, Lispector escalates the tension inherent in the story's basic conflict (which resides in Anna's personality) by noting through the third-person narrative voice that for Anna the "dangerous" part of the day was the afternoon, "when the house was empty and she was no longer needed" (39). Although the reader knows of Anna's secret inner fear, that of not being "needed," of not being "in control," her character is developed externally, by means of her external or social being. During the crucial second part of the story, which begins when Anna suddenly sees a blind man chewing gum and ends as she finally returns to her apartment, Anna's "external" mode of existence is sharply contrasted with her "internal" existence. Anna, we learn, has tried to control her fears (of chaos and futility) by flawlessly performing her daily domestic duties: dusting the furniture, cooking the meals, doing the laundry, mending, and going shopping.

Anna is seen sighing with "satisfaction," then, as she is returning home to her secure, "controlled" world from yet another successful shopping trip. But then the unexpected happens, the seemingly trivial event that completely undoes Anna's carefully structured but inherently false (and therefore fragile) world. This, the moment when Anna's eyes fall upon the blind man chewing gum, amounts to an epiphany for her, an event that sets off a chain reaction of moments of intense, lyrically expressed inner revelation. The structure of the story helps set off the contrast between Anna's psychic condition before the discovery of the blind man and her condition afterwards. Just as the streetcar itself physically jolts and jars along, so too does Anna's mind, suddenly thrown off balance, begin to reel in its quickening realization that it is becoming involved in a situation—an experience—over which it has no control and in which Anna herself will be of minor importance. As the narrative voice records this process for the reader, we note that "suddenly she saw the man stationary at the tram stop . . . blind. . . . Something disquieting was happening. Then she discovered what it was: the blind man was chewing gum . . ." (39–40).

In a sudden contrast between Anna's now disintegrating inner world, formerly so organized and controlled, and her external appearance (a contrast deftly achieved by means of a change in the story's point of view at this juncture), we learn that "Anna stared at him as if he had insulted her. And anyone watching would have received the impression of a woman filled with hatred" (40). With the reference here to "hate," a reference made in regard to a woman whose existence, she feels, is based on "love," Clarice Lispector strikes what is for her an ironic motif of her work, the constant and integral interplay of love and hate in human life, a feature of her fiction that dominates the story "The Buffalo" (*Family Ties*).

Utterly disoriented by her sudden and unexpected experience, Anna accidentally drops and breaks the eggs she has been carrying with her. In a key phrase, one trenchant in its irony, we learn that although "a few moments later people were no longer staring at her, the damage had been done" (40). Referring to both the breaking of the eggs and the breaking of Anna's spuriously secure existence, this line subtly ties together the story's two spheres of "action"—the outer (the incidental event) and the inner (Anna's tumultuous reaction to it).

Realizing that some kind of personal crisis has come, and that "a blind man chewing gum had plunged the world into a mysterious excitement" (41), Anna suddenly feels (like Sartre's Roquentine and Camus's Meursault) that "life was filled to the brim with a sickening nausea" (42). Although Lispector has stated that her nausea is not the nausea of Sartre,[19] her sense of the world suddenly becoming suffocating and disgusting in its chaotic extravagance clearly recalls the existential world described by Sartre and Camus.[20]

Desperate, now, to escape somehow from the terror and, paradoxically, the "compassion" (42) that are overwhelming her, Anna stumbles off the tram at the wrong stop, at the Botanical Garden. Linking here the archetypal force of the primitive world (this constituting yet another motif of the author's work) to Anna's nascent, primitive consciousness (or to what is about to become such), the reader learns that "everything seemed strange, much too gentle, much too great" (43). Then, utilizing the lyrical ambiguity that is so fundamental a part of her expressive style, Lispector connects the natural power of the Botanical Garden with what has happened to Anna's former sense of identity: "The rawness of the world was peaceful. The murder was deep. And death was not what one had imagined" (43). The "murder" referred to is that of Anna's false sense of who she was, a "murder" perpetrated by the primitive authenticity of the natural world in the garden. Paradoxically referring to death as "not what one had imagined," Lispector calls attention to a crucial point; what has "died" (been "murdered") was the fundamental meretriciousness of Anna's old life, her false existence. But "death" has been replaced by "life," by a new, higher, and now, finally, "authentic" (in existential terms) realization about herself, if only Anna will accept it. Structurally, the remainder of the story is concerned with how Anna handles this situation, with what choice she will ultimately make about her future.

Having taken Anna to this crucial moment, Lispector moves quickly to remove her from the natural world of the garden and return her to her former world, one now depicted as being in complete conflict with the garden. Remembering her children (the primary reasons she would have to return to her former life, in part or in whole), Anna regains her senses (her conventional middle-class mentality?) and runs back to her apartment building and the rooms that constituted the heart of her external world. But, suggesting that she has been irremediably altered by her experience in the garden, she asks herself, as she goes into her apartment, "What new land was this? And for a moment that wholesome life she had led until today seemed morally crazy." Now, paradoxically and perhaps as a different woman, "she loved with loathing" (44).

Encountering one of her children and her husband, neither of whom are named but who are referred to generically, Anna suddenly and again unexpectedly is confronted with a deeply disruptive challenge to her self-consciousness; this situation ironically parallels that of the blind man on the tram because while that scene involved Anna's departure from her bourgeois mentality, the discovery of her husband and one of her children marks her return (now perhaps changed) to it. At this juncture, then, Anna utters some words that are oddly inexpressive of the confused but intense inner state that generates them. Or, to put the problem into another perspective, Anna's spoken words, her dialogues especially, fail to convey the intensity that her unspoken words have. Typical of Lispector's treatment of dialogue (which, for her, is consistently ambiguous, cryptic, and deeply arcane) and monologue (usually silent, allusive, and associational in its search for ultimate truths), what Anna says aloud is contrasted to the silent verbalizations of the turmoil she is feeling. Thus she says to her now confused and frightened child, "Life is horrible. . . . I am afraid. . . . Don't let Mummy forget you" (45).

Paralleling the "secret life" of the Botanical Garden, a flower in her apartment makes Anna realize that "the same secret activity was going on here in the kitchen," that all around her was "a silent, slow, insistent life" (46). Horrified by this sudden realization that her citadel of domestic tranquillity and order had been breached by the disruptive force of primitive life, Anna "went from one side of the kitchen to the other, cutting the steaks, mixing the cream" (46). Then, at the moment of her greatest suffering, when (ironically) "faith broke her" (46), Anna's dinner guests arrive, thus "requiring" her full attention and thereby saving her from the throes of continued inner anguish. Reengaged in her comfortable role of mother, wife, and hostess, Anna's former world begins to establish its primacy for her once again. Although (to the others) Anna looks a "little pale," she "laughed gently with the others" now (47). Superficially, at least, things have returned to "normal." But have they? Is everything as it had been before?

Later that evening, when her guests have left, Anna wonders to herself, "Would the experience unleashed by the blind man fill her days?" (47). Having verbalized the crux of the issue, Anna continues to ponder the ambiguous meaning of her experience: "How many years would it take before she once more grew old? . . . But with the ill-will of a lover, she seemed to accept that the fly would emerge from the flower, and the giant water lilies would float in the darkness of the lake. The blind man was hanging among the fruits of the botanical garden" (47).

Virtually at the conclusion of the tale, when the reader, responding to the text, must try to decide whether Anna has changed or not, and whether she will become a "new person" or remain a timid, dependent bourgeoise who accepts the demeaning identity parceled out to her by a system of social stereotypes, Lispector has Anna say something that, in its ambiguity, sums up her own confused feelings about what has happened to her that day. Hearing a noise coming from her stove, a reference to which had opened the story, Anna asks, "What happened?" (37). But while the external object of this question is clearly the stove (Anna's husband, who exists in a state of complete ignorance of his wife's inner anguish, succinctly demonstrates this for us), the internal referent is Anna's psychic revelation. Lispector makes us feel the irony of this situation by writing, "This afternoon, something tranquil had exploded, and in the house everything struck a tragicomic note" (47).

Lispector brings the story to an end, then, on a perfectly balanced note of ambiguity, a structural feature that is fully characteristic of her best work: was Anna going to become a new person, one who assumed full responsibility for her being, one vitalized by Sartrean "good faith," or was she going to return to her orthodox, middle-class domesticity? Because Lispector herself has Anna's ironically uncomprehending husband (he is physically close to her but psychically distant) lead her off to bed, thereby "removing her from the danger of living" (47), one is left with the impression that Anna will retreat into dependence and conventionality, that although she had had her liberating experience she cannot, or will not, bear its burden of personal responsibility. Anna has seen the face of freedom in the primitive forces of the garden and she has turned away from it, not being strong enough or not willing to assume full responsibility for living a new, free, and demanding identity. In one aspect, Anna's torment would be doubly poignant; having seen freedom but having rejected it out of a sense of uncertainty, she would live out her life in the solitude and isolation that come from fear and not from freedom. Read in this context, Anna's story becomes an ironic and sad parable of the human experience.

In "A explicação inútil" ("The Useless Explanation"), Lispector wrote that she identified intensely with Anna,[21] a fact that reminds us of how frequently autobiographical elements find their way into Lispector's fiction. "Love," an ironic yet lyrically wrought tale that features a tightly knit internal structure based on an epiphanylike moment of revelation, can be taken as a model of the kind of short fiction that Lispector wrote. One of her most famous and respected stories, "Love" is one of her most finely crafted pieces as well.

Another outstanding selection from this landmark collection— and one that, given Lispector's marital situation at the time, may be read as a partially autobiographical piece—is "Family Ties," the story of a woman whose realization of self puts her at odds with the people and social structures around her. Reflecting this dual conflict (one individual and one social), "Family Ties" divides itself into two levels of action: in the first one, Catarina, the main character, and her mother nearly overcome the breach between them and succeed in communicating. But at the critical moment, words fail to break their solitude and the hesitant effort falls short. Each woman goes her separate way, except that Catarina has mysteriously transformed the "painful love that seemed to her happiness" (*Alguns contos*, 14) into a positive, self-liberating force. She returns home, sizes up her situation (which the reader learns about, in a dramatic change of perspective, through the eyes of the woman's husband), takes her child by the hand, and goes out. In their authentic, "nonsocialized" condition the woman and the child seem to become coconspirators in a self-conscious act of liberation, that of leaving their apartment. The delicate yet powerfully suggestive question is how long do they leave; forever, or only to "take a walk"? Ironically, however, the man, in his superficial way, realizes that the love that ties the family together (including mother and son) may also make each one of them a "prisoner of love," denying them individual freedom. This ironic, double-edged view of love becomes one of Lispector's most basic themes. It plays a role, directly or indirectly, in nearly all of the author's stories and, in the novel *Uma aprendizagem ou o livro dos prazeres,* would be developed into the basic organizing force of the entire work.

Suggestive and often nebulous, the stories of *Alguns contos* are compelling in their intensely human portrayal of the drama of existence. As well crafted and subtle as they are, however, they are only a prelude to Lispector's next collection of short stories.

Laços de família (1960)

Composed of thirteen stories (six of which had appeared in *Alguns contos*), *Laços de família* was one of the most original and powerful books of its time in Latin America. Seen in retrospect, the enigmatic but luminous tales of *Laços de família* are as distinctive as were those of the early Julio Cortázar. One could say, in fact, that just as Borges and Cortázar came to revolutionize the way short fiction was to be written in Spanish America, so, too, did Clarice Lispector help to revolutionize the short-story form in Brazil. Perhaps Lispector's most successful and satisfying collection of stories, *Laços de família* offers ample proof that their author can be considered a master of the modern short story.

As in the earlier anthology, *Alguns contos,* the pieces that make up *Laços de família* are structured around the epiphany. A story such as the delicate and poised "Preciousness," for example, is not so much about an event or action as it is about the sensations of confusion, fear, and anxiety that well up in the mind of a young girl who, going through puberty, has an unspecified experience with some boys. With characteristic ambiguity and tension, Lispector orchestrates the decisive event of the story in such a way that the reader does not know for certain exactly what did or did not happen. But in the girl's mind, which is where the drama of the story exists, the event is seen by the reader as being a traumatic one, one that significantly alters her sense of self.

Another story from this landmark collection, "The Crime of the Mathematics Professor," is one of Lispector's most famous works.[22] Dealing with the themes of guilt, punishment, and expiation, the narrative tells the story of a man who, by burying (only to exhume

at the conclusion of the story) a stray dog he has found dead in the
street, hopes to atone for having once abandoned another dog. Biblical in its symbolism and parablelike in its tone, "The Crime of the
Mathematics Professor" numbers among Lispector's most challenging tales.

The final tale of the collection is "The Buffalo," a story that
brilliantly depicts Lispector's ambivalent and contrastive attitudes
about love and hate. This well-known story also shows Lispector's
skillful use of animals as primitive creatures who mirror, in their
own living but mute way, our own notions of being. A third feature
of this tale, and one that links it to "Family Ties," is Lispector's
concept of feminism, which rests on the basic premise that strength
and independence can come about only through self-awareness.

"The Buffalo" focuses on an unnamed woman who, spurned in
love, turns unexpectedly but resolutely to hate in order to affirm
herself, to establish a state of prideful self-awareness. Because her
entire sense of purpose in the world had been based around a vision
of herself as a provider of "love" for others, her embracing of hatred
amounts to an act of self-affirmation in the face of having had her
offer of "love" devastatingly rejected by a man.

The possessive, potentially deforming impulses toward both love
and hate that live within the woman make it difficult for her to
keep the two feelings separate and manageable. We learn from the
third-person limited point of view that puts the reader "inside" the
woman's mind: "Então, nascida do ventre, de novo subiu, inplor-
ante, em onda vagarosa a vontade de matar—seus olhos molharam-
se gratos e negros numa quase felicidade, não era o ódio ainda, por
enquanto apenas a vontade atormentada de ódio como um desejo,
a promessa do desabrochamento cruel, um tormento como de amor,
a vontade de ódio se prometendo sagrado sangue e triunfo, a fêmea
rejeitada espiritualizara-se na grande esperança. . . . Onde aprender a odiar para não morrer de amor?"[23] (Rising from her womb,
there comes once more, imploring and in a slow wave, the urge to
destroy. Her eyes moistened, grateful and black, in something near
to happiness. It was not yet hatred; as yet it was only the tortured
will to hate possessing her like some desire, the promise of a cruel
flowering, a torment as of love, the craving for hatred promising
itself sacred blood and triumph, and the spurned female had spir-
itualized herself in great expectancy. . . . Where would she learn
to hate so as not to die of love?)

Moving through the zoo in search of the right animal through whom she could give vent to her torment, the woman encounters the buffalo. At this point the iron bars of the cage that have seemed to keep the animals away from the people, paralleling a subtle shift in the story's perspective, now seem to keep the woman imprisoned, isolating her from the buffalo. Connecting viscerally with the buffalo's primitive presence (in a way reminiscent of Cortázar's Mexican salamanders in "Axolotl"), the woman swoons under the weight of her epiphany and falls unconscious to the ground.

Judged as a whole the stories of *Laços de família* rank among the very best produced by a Latin American author in the mid-twentieth century. Written with great economy of style and focusing relentlessly on the inner drama of human beings undergoing some kind of disruptive experience, the stories of *Laços de família* established Clarice Lispector as a major force in Brazilian narrative, especially the story form.

A *legião estrangeira* (1964)

Published in the same year as the novel *A paixão segundo G. H.*, Lispector's third book of stories continues to chart the development of minds that suddenly and unexpectedly discover both themselves and the world, a world full of similarly conscious but isolated beings. More than in *Laços de família*, the pieces in *A legião estrangeira* often reflect a new kind of awareness of the existential condition. Within this general new trend toward an intensely personal discovery of truth about one's own private human condition, a trend that may be said to constitute a motif of the book, are several pieces that expand on themes and topics touched on in earlier works.

One of these pieces, for example, "Viagem a Petrópolis" (Journey to Petropolis), deals, among other things, with the sociopsychological problems of old age, a theme that Lispector would return to in other works. Similar, in some respects, to the old family matriarch of "Feliz aniversário" (Happy birthday), the old woman of "Viagem a Petrópolis" does not realize just how alone and isolated she is. The first line of the story suggests that the old woman's dilemma is social in nature, and in truth it is: "Era uma velha sequinha que, doce e obstinada, não parecia compreender que estava só no mundo"[24] (She was a dried-up old woman who, sweet and obstinate, didn't seem to understand that she was alone in the world). Essentially cast off by a younger and materialistic society, the old woman is presented as being irrelevant to it; serving no real purpose, she seeks shelter and care wherever she can find it. Simultaneously pathetic and ridiculous, the old woman, asked to leave the house in which she has been staying, suddenly but calmly realizes her superfluous condition. When she does this, she dies, death ironically becoming the outward manifestation of her inner experience, her realization that she was not only alone in the world, but a pariah. As with most of Lispector's other characters, this realization is shattering; with the old woman, however, it is received in a quiescent, even fatalistic way not unlike the hen in "Uma galinha" ("The Chicken") of *Laços de família.*

Another tale from *A legião estrangeira* that organizes itself around the motif of existential self-discovery is "Sofia's Disasters," the story about a schoolgirl who, because her teacher shows a sincere interest in an unusual story she has written, comes to learn about the pleasure and pain of love. Told from the girl's perspective, the story of what happened (a trivial comment) is reflected in the tangled but impassioned mind of the girl. And while she admits she does not "understand" what had taken place—that is, her moment of revelation, of transformation—she knows that somehow she has been forever changed. Almost an extension of "Mystery in São Cristóvão," Sofia declares to herself at the end of her story, "E foi assim que no grande parque do colégio lentamente comecei a aprender a ser amada, suportando o sacrifício de não merecer, apenas para suavizar a dor de quem não ama. Não, esse foi sòmente um dos motivos. É que os outros fazem outras histórias. Em algumas foi de meu coração que outras garras cheias de duro amor arrancaram a flecha farpada, e sem nojo de meu grito"[25] (Thus it was that in the large park of the school I slowly began to learn how to be loved, while bearing the pain of one who does not love. No, that was only one of the motives. The others form other stories. In some, other claws swollen with cruel love pulled the barbed arrows from my heart without feeling nauseated from my screams).

A third selection of *A legião estrangeira,* "A quinta história," ranks among the most structurally unusual of Lispector's early pieces. Less than five pages long, the story is really composed of four separate but connected narratives; a fifth one exists in the text as a title, "Leibnitz e a transcendência do amor na Polinésia" (Leibnitz and the transcendency of love in Polynesia), and with the same beginning that the other "stories" have, "queixei-me de baratas" (I complained about cockroaches). Because although even in its acute brevity this "fifth story" begins as the other four do, the reader senses that this final piece also deals with cockroaches in a way that connects it to what the other four have discussed. Upon finishing "A quinta história" the reader can look back at the rest of the tale and see how the entire work must be read in the same way that the segment entitled "fifth story" is integrated by the reader's own imagination into the framework formed by the preceding pieces, each of which could stand on its own as a separate, if short, story. Though perhaps too abrupt in its transitions from text to text, "A quinta história's" imaginative structuring shows Clarice Lispector seeking new ways of involving the reader in the interpretation of her open, ironically designed texts. "A quinta história," along with several others in *A legião estrangeira* (and elsewhere), offers much interesting material for the reader interested in deconstructionist theory and criticism as well as that of much reader response theory.

Felicidade clandestina (1971)

Although this rather extensive collection of stories contains twenty-five pieces, only nine of them had not been published elsewhere earlier. Of the new stories, the title tale, "Felicidade clandestina" (Clandestine happiness), is typical of Lispector's efforts in this, her fourth anthology of short fictions. "Felicidade clandestina" tells the story of how a tall, graceful girl is imaginatively tormented by a short, fat girl. Ironic in its conception, this basic conflict develops because of a single fact: the unattractive girl (who did not care for them) had access to books, which were desperately sought after by the attractive girl. The former, whose father was the owner of a bookshop, would, in a carefully calculated act of apparent kindness, offer to supply books to the tall, pretty girl. But each time the latter, full of excitement and anticipation would journey to the house of the short, fat girl, she would be told that, for a variety of reasons, the book was not available to her at that time. This cruel game went on for some time until one day the short, fat girl's mother noticed what was happening and forced her daughter to loan the book to the other girl.

The tall, pretty girl then takes the book, portrayed as a sacred object, home with her to enjoy in private. Her "enjoyment" of it, however, ironically consists of her imagining that a variety of problems were preventing her from reading it, from achieving the state of "happiness" that reading it would give her. As the narrative voice, that of the girl seeking the book, declares, "Criava as mais falsas dificuldades para aquela coisa clandestina que era a felicidade. A felicidade sempre iria ser clandestina para mim"[26] (I was creating the most false difficulties for that clandestine thing that was happiness. Happiness would always be clandestine for me). In the final line of the story, the reader sees how the girl's "clandestine happiness" has erotically and mysteriously converted her into a woman and the book into a "lover," the object of her love.

The ambiguity of the ending ties this story to several other tales in *Felicidade clandestina,* in particular the pieces entitled "Macacos" ("Marmosets"), "O ôvo e a galinha" (The egg and the chicken [which was presented by Lispector at the 1976 World Witchcraft Congress in Bogotá]),[27] and "As águas do mundo" (The waters of the world [which is remarkable for showing how Lispector could make use of archetypes in her fiction; this latter text was earlier a chapter of the novel *Uma aprendizagem ou o livro dos prazeres*]). In "Macacos," however, Lispector brings into play several of her most basic motifs: children (portrayed as elementary human beings capable of systematic and protracted cruelty), animals (primitive, preverbal beings), irony and ambiguity, acute psychological tension, feminism and love.

"Macacos" ("Marmosets," trans. Elizabeth Bishop) is really two stories: in the first one, a male marmoset, addressed as a "man," momentarily comes into the life of a mother and her children; in the second one, the mother buys another marmoset, a female, named Lisette. Lisette, already sick, begins to die, however, and only by regularly giving her oxygen can she be kept alive. These treatments, described as "um sopro de vida" ("a breath of life"), make one wonder if Lispector did not have this story in mind when writing her final work, the novel *Um sopro de vida.* The treatments are in vain, however, and Lisette finally dies, whereupon the narrator's older son says that she, his mother, "looks so much like Lisette!"[28] In response to this comment, but with wider-ranging implications, the narrator delivers the final ambiguous and ironic line of the story: "Eu também gosto de você . . ."[29] (I love you, too . . . trans. E. E. Fitz). Although Bishop rendered the verb "gosto" as "like," which is indeed a plausible translation, the stronger verb "love" seems more in keeping with Lispector's previous usages of the term, especially as put forth in *Laços de família* (see "Love," "Family Ties," and "The Buffalo" [trans. G. Pontiero]).

As in so much of her work, Lispector appears to be partially autobiographical in these stories. The book in question in "Felicidade clandestina," for example, is *As reinações de Narizinho,* by Monteiro Lobato, a work known to have been one of Lispector's childhood favorites. A corollary to what might be termed the autobiographicality of these stories is Lispector's tendency to refer in her fiction to other stories and novels she has written. The phrase "um sopro de vida" is an example of this, as is the use of the name Lisette for the little animal of "Macacos." This name (and, apparently, this animal) is referred to in the "children's" story "A mulher que matou as peixes" as having been one of Lispector's real pets.

In general, the new stories of *Felicidade clandestina* show Lispector continuing as she had begun with *Alguns contos* in 1952. Different, however, are her more studied ambiguity, her ever sharper sense of irony, and her increasingly "political" (if often symbolic) commentaries on women and old people in late-twentieth-century urban society. *Felicidade clandestina* shows how Lispector was growing as an artist, but doing so without ever abandoning her characteristic themes or her singular style.[30]

A imitação da rosa (1973)

This is a collection of what were judged to be some of Lispector's best stories, all of which had been previously published.

Onde estivestes de noite (1974)

Though normally classified as "fiction," *Onde estivestes de noite* contains several pieces, such as "*O manifesto da cidade*" (The manifest of the city), "Silêncio" (Silence, a recurring motif in Lispector's work), "Tanta Mansidão" (Such gentleness), and "Tempestade de Almas" (Storm of souls), which are more personal or philosophical reflection than story. Other narratives, such as "O relatório da coisa" (The telling about the thing), "O morto no mar da Urca" (The dead boy in the surf at Urca), and "É para lá que eu vou" (It's over there that I'm going), are hybrid pieces, part story and part introspective commentary by Lispector herself. More clearly stories are "A procura de uma dignidade" (The search for dignity), "A partida do trem"

(The train's departure), "Uma tarde plena" (One late afternoon), and "Onde estivestes de noite" (Where you were last night).

"Onde estivestes de noite," a mysterious and poetic tale involving mythological and androgynous life-forces, deals with what is perhaps Lispector's most fundamental theme—the psychological process of becoming, of experiencing an inner and not necessarily permanent transformation. Full of references to things, to animals (especially horses, another of Lispector's favorite motifs), people, and inanimate objects, the story incorporates other of Lispector's characteristic motifs: silence, love and hate, pain, language (always portrayed as a vital and creative though flawed life-force itself), and darkness. Additionally, there is also a note of wry humor as the narrator observes at one point how a certain person believed he was making a political statement by eating Danish caviar rather than Russian caviar.

Another story from this collection, "A procura de uma identidade," is more concretely portrayed than the metaphoric and speculative "Onde estivestes de noite." "A procura de uma dignidade" concerns a moment in the life of a woman, Mrs. Jorge B. Xavier, who is lost in the labyrinthine corridors underneath the huge football stadium of Maracanã. Geographically lost, the woman slowly and timidly begins to perceive that she is also psychologically lost, that just as she cannot find one of the stadium's exit doors neither can she see any way out of what she fearfully suspects has been a false, inauthentic, and trivial life. The two planes of the story, the physical or geographic and the psychological, merge in the story's final line, as the woman desperately yearns for "a way out" of her frustrated and fantasy-filled existence.

By focusing on a nearly sixty-year-old woman, one who has spent a lifetime defining herself in terms of her husband and her social status, Lispector calls our attention to one of her often overlooked themes—the social and psychological problems of old age. Living in a society infatuated with material things and youth, a nonyouthful person may come to realize that a life spent only in pursuit of material things is a shallow, wasted life. Should this realization about the relative importance of things occur late in life, as it does with Mrs. Jorge B. Xavier, the result can be sensations of desperation and anguish, these being the principal emotions experienced by the feckless and dependent protagonist of "A procura de uma dignidade."

In general, the selections that make up *Onde estivestes de noite* continue to explore Lispector's basic themes, the essential isolation of human beings, the failure of language to break us out of our solitude, and the urgent need we feel to find what is most crucial to our sense of being, to know who and what we are. *Onde estivestes de noite* is different, however, in that many of its tales rely on a subtle ironic humor to make this point. Told predominantly through an often self-conscious first-person narration and occasionally concerning characters who, like Ângela Pralini of "A partida do trem," reappear in later works (*Um sopro de vida*), the short stories and commentaries of *Onde estivestes de noite* show their author experimenting with new themes, forms, and modes of expression. But these experiments are carried out without Lispector's abandoning the basic themes, forms, and modes of expression that had, ever since 1944, made her one of Latin America's most respected narrativists.

A via crucis do corpo (1974)

Published in the same year as *Onde estivestes de noite*, *A via crucis do corpo* is notable among Lispector's work for three reasons: (1) the degree to which it openly invites the reader to construct and then deconstruct the text, (2) the frankness of its sexuality, and (3) the reduced number of stories that focus on the inner process of a character's nascent sense of identity.

Eroticism, a restrained but omnipresent force in Lispector's fiction,[31] develops into an open sexuality in several of the stories in *A via crucis do corpo*. It does so, however, both sensually and comically, the latter feature reflecting an increasingly significant aspect of Lispector's post-1960 work. Love, portrayed more often carnally in these stories than philosophically or psychologically, also emerges finally as a thematic and structural characteristic in this collection.

One of the best illustrations of the new treatment that love gets in *A via crucis do corpo* is the story "Miss Algrave." This is the rather droll tale of a single woman who, living the life of a reclusive ascetic in London, is visited by an extraterrestrial being from Saturn. This creature, who goes by the name IXTLAN, makes love to her and thereby awakens her to a more satisfying and vital level of existence, one that is both physical and psychological in its appeal. Miss Algrave quits her typist job and becomes a prostitute in order to while away the hours until her true love, IXTLAN, can make one of his periodic visits to see her.

Another story of this sort, one with powerful elements of irony, sexual violence, and social hypocrisy in it, is "O corpo" (The body), the story of Xavier, a bigamist who lived with two women, Carmem and Beatriz. The two women, sad lovers as well as friends, are obsessed by Xavier. As their relationship begins to deteriorate, which it does because of Xavier's inconstancy to them, Carmem and Beatriz conspire to kill him, which they do. Eventually the crime is discovered, but rather than arrest the two women the police, anxious to avoid a lot of paperwork and trouble, tell them to pack their bags for Montevideo and never come back. The women say "thank you" and leave, ending the story.

Two stories of a less overtly sexual nature are "O homem que apareceu" ("The Man Who Appeared," trans. Alexis Levitin), another possibly autobiographical story about a chance meeting between a divorced woman writer and a man on the street, and "Melhor do que arder" ("Better Than to Burn," trans. Alexis Levitin), a gently ironic tale of a woman who leaves a convent in order to find peace, fulfillment, and happiness through marriage to a man, not a god.

A *via crucis do corpo* was the last collection of stories published by Clarice Lispector before her death in 1977. When compared to her other story collections, it is notable for presenting at times a Clarice Lispector very different from the one the readers had come to know. This "new" Clarice Lispector is seen in such stories as "A linguagem do 'P,' " "Miss Algrave," "O corpo," and "Via crucis," a tale of extended irony that parallels Christ's virgin birth while suggesting in its pungent conclusion, that in undergoing the struggles and travails of this life everyone travels "the way of the cross."

The title of the collection itself suggests a fundamentally ironic cast to the stories included in it. In terms of individual men and women, the way of the cross both begins and ends in the flesh, that is, in the enigma of the human condition. Sex, ordinarily felt to be profane, can be a sacred act; and the supposedly sacred life of a convent nun may actually be profane. In the end, perhaps only love both of the flesh and of the spirit can get us through the real "via crucis," that is the human experience.

Written with smoothness and concison and reinforced with irony and sardonic humor, many of the pieces of A *via crucis do corpo* rank among Lispector's most successful and satisfying efforts as a short-story writer. Only *Laços de família,* with its overall excellence, can be said critically to rank ahead of the narratives of *A via crucis do corpo.* Coming as they did at the end of Lispector's career as a writer of short fiction, tales such as "Miss Algrave," "O corpo," and "Via crucis" prove both the depth of Lispector's creativity and the enduring originality of her voice.

A bela e a fera (1979)

This work, compiled and organized by Lispector's friend and companion Olga Borelli, is very useful to the reader who wishes to see how Lispector developed as a story writer. The first six stories of the collection were written when Lispector was an adolescent. She was fourteen, in fact, when, showing a truly precocious talent for writing, she composed "História interrompida" (An interrupted story). These early stories had never appeared in print before their publicaton in *A bela e a fera;* Lispector had kept them in a desk drawer for nearly forty years. The last two stories of the collection were the last two ever written by Lispector and, like the anthology's first six pieces, had not been published before appearing in *A bela e a fera,* a title that was picked especially for this collection by Lispector's son Paulo Gurgel Valente.

Because it includes some of Lispector's earliest short fiction as well as her final efforts in this form, *A bela e a fera* offers the reader a rare opportunity to compare and contrast work done at the beginning and end of her career. What is startling here is how controlled and perceptive Lispector was as a fledgling author of fourteen.

The other five narratives that form part 1 of the collection, are generally similar in style and tone. There are moments of conventionality and superficiality, of course, and instances of awkward phrasings and transitions, but taken as a whole these early narratives are truly remarkable for their ability to isolate and focus on both physical details and psychological states. Many of Lispector's basic motifs, moreover, such as self-awareness, silence, language, and the marking of time by psychologically apprehended "moments," are already playing central roles in these early tales.

The last two stories show, as one would expect, a smoother, more powerfully focused style, one that effectively combines irony and archness with the poignant flashes of political and psychic insight into her characters that the reader expects to find in the mature Clarice Lispector. Because of the unique way she went about composing her narratives, however, it is difficult to say with any degree of confidence how thoroughly she herself controlled or directed the growth in technical sophistication and thematic depth that we sense in the later pieces. In terms of their style and content, Lispector's last two stories are more complete than the earlier ones and therefore more satisfying. But there can be no doubt that the early pieces, one of which, "História interrompida," dates from 1939, held great promise for their author, a promise that was many times fulfilled.

* * *

O mistério do coelho pensante
(uma estória policial para crianças) (1967)

Lispector's children's stories came about because one day while living in Washington, D.C., her youngest son, Paulo, asked his mother why, being a writer, she had never written any stories for children. Apparently touched by this question, Lispector composed a tale, *O mistério do coelho pensante,* based on her recollection of some pet rabbits she and her two children had once owned.

In a short prolegomenon to the work Lispector explains that she deliberately left the work "open" so that each reader might fill in between the lines as he or she saw fit. She also states that the "mystery" of the title is really more of a *conversa íntima* ("intimate conversation") than a "story" per se. The story is therefore potentially more extensive than its actual number of pages would indicate.

These words can, as in all of Lispector's fiction, be read in more than one way. Here, for example, her carefully worded preparatory note to the reader can be taken as an innocent explanation of a children's story, with the term "children's story" used in its commonly understood sense—that is, as a simple story designed to entertain children. But because the words of the preface are not only open to other interpretations but suggestive of them, a politically conscious reader might well respond to them as constituting a subtle invitation to read or "construct" the story in a sharply political fashion.

This latter possibility is given more credence when one remembers Lispector's personal political consciousness, her participation in street demonstrations, and the fact that the story was published in 1967, three years after the April 1, 1964, coup that placed a military dictatorship in power in Brazil.

Read strictly as juvenile literature, the story is a simple one: a pet rabbit, Joãozinho, is kept in a little hutch covered by a heavy metal lid. One day he decides that he will escape from the cage any time he is not given enough to eat. He does so one day, but is captured and returned to his cage. The "mystery," as the narrative voice (which seems to be that of Lispector herself) tells us, is that it is not known how Joãozinho got out. The rabbit then begins to escape more and more, not for a lack of food but because he has acquired a taste for getting out. Eventually he begins to escape simply to look around, to see "how things were." It is at this time (this level of his development) that he becomes a *coelho pensante* (a "thinking rabbit").

If read on another level, one that would sustain the notion that, in 1967, Lispector wanted her readers to think about what was happening to Brazil, four moments in the narrative emerge as crucial: (1) that rabbits (like middle-class citizens?) do not "think about things" and that this makes them "happy";[32] (2) that as long as the rabbits (the middle class?) had enough to eat, they would not try to escape (change the political regime and the social order) (12); (3) that the more Joãozinho (each individual) escaped from his cage (life under a dictatorship), the more he wanted to do it (when political freedoms are taken away, people yearn for them all the more ardently) (14); and (4) that when Joãozinho began to escape (rebel) because he wanted to see "how things were" (to discover the truth about the dictatorship), he became a "thinking rabbit" (a politically aware citizen) (20).

There is no hard textual evidence anywhere in the story that will either confirm or deny this politically sensitive reading of *O mistério do coelho pensante*. The time of its writing, the author's own political views, and the poised ambiguities of the four key moments in the narration all make a political interpretation of this story possible, however. And this, given the mysterious relationship between human events and the ability of language to "reconstruct" and "deconstruct" them, is sufficient. It is enough to say that *O mistério do coelho pensante* can be read this way, for the possibility enhances the story's appeal. A reader trained in the "reader response" school of criticism, deconstructionism or in literary hermeneutics might find this "children's story" of considerable interest. Recalling Lispector's admonitions in the preface about how each reader would have to supply the "between the lines" information,[33] it certainly seems at least possible that Clarice Lispector's motives in writing *O mistério do coelho pensante* were partly political as well as familial. At any rate, this story, and *A mulher que matou os peixes,* rank together as the two most "serious" and socially thought provoking of Lispector's four volumes of children's material.

A mulher que matou os peixes (1968)

The second of Lispector's "children's stories," *A mulher que matou os peixes,* is a story about a woman who gets so busy with her work that she forgets to feed some fish that have been left in her care. Unfed for three days, the fish die of hunger. The narrative's voice, which, because of several details revealed in the text, again seems to be that of Clarice Lispector herself, asks, even begs a group of children for "forgiveness" for having committed this "crime."

Because the words *crime* ("crime"), *culpa* ("guilt"), and *perdão* ("pardon") play such prominent roles in the text, and because the story opens and closes with the voice seeking forgiveness for her "crime," the reader is reminded of a very similar, though more "adult" story, "O crime do professor de matemática." There is, in both stories, a note of anguish in the words spoken by the narrative voice. And while the narrator's tone in *A mulher que matou os peixes* is more muted than the professor's tone, the reader senses a real note of desperation in it. There is, in other words, an intensity and a seriousness to *A mulher que matou os peixes* that is lacking in a great deal of the pabulum that often passes for "children's literature."

Beyond the fact that the fish die of starvation, there are other examples of the violence of the real world in Lispector's tale; a pet dog is torn to pieces by a pack of dogs, people eat rabbits and ducks, and animals (a monkey named Lisete, for example; see "Macacos") get sick and die. Like the Old World version of such tales as "Little Red Riding Hood" the sobering verisimilitude of Lispector's story suggests that the author wants children (and adults) to take it seriously. Though simplified stylistically, *A mulher que matou os peixes,* like Lispector's other "children's stories," makes a statement about how the world of human beings really is. If not always pretty and happy, *A mulher que matou os peixes* has the ring of truth to it.

A *vida íntima de Laura* (1974)

Lispector's third attempt at children's literature is considerably more of an orthodox "children's story" than her previous two efforts.[34] *A vida íntima de Laura* concerns the "intimate life" of Laura, a simple-minded red and brown barnyard chicken. Married to Luís, Laura's life centers around the laying of eggs (a task at which she is at first very good) and eating (an activity at which she also is very accomplished). The tranquillity of Laura's life is broken, however, by five events: the birth of a chick; a thief's attempt to steal her; being loaned out to a neighboring chicken farm; having the household cook suggest to her employer that Laura (who was said to be getting old and no longer a good layer of eggs) be killed and eaten; and finally a visit from Xert, a one-eyed chicken-sized visitor from Jupiter who tells Laura that she is never going to be killed and eaten because he will not permit it. Earlier in their conversation Laura had confided in Xert that if her destiny was to be eaten, she would like to be eaten by Pelé, Brazil's great soccer player.

The story of Laura who, in her "intimate life," recalls the chicken-protagonist of the story "A galinha," also has some enigmatic references to subjects more serious than the private life of a chicken. The social problem of racism is broached when the narrator, who seems to be Lispector herself, mentions that hens like Laura, who constituted the majority, did not belittle another, different hen, one who was of a different size and color. The narrator also observes how adults, in their oddly paradoxical and contradictory way, can both love live chickens (as she does) and love to eat them. The narrator also has Laura, who is about to explain to Xert what humans are like "inside," say that they are very complicated, that sometimes they even feel themselves obliged to lie.

Although one might be tempted to read the story of Laura as the story of women in Brazil, the overall tone and structure of the story do not seem to warrant this interpretation. Rather, the story of Laura, beyond the personal relevancy a particular reader may derive from it, really seems meant more as pure diversion than political commentary. Read in this fashion, then *A vida íntima de Laura* seems less "politically conscious" than *A mulher que matou os peixes* and, especially, *O mistério do coelho pensante*.

The "children's stories" of Clarice Lispector pose some interesting questions for readers who identify with the "deconstructionist" school of literary criticism. Are Lispector's "children's stories" meant only as pure diversion for young people or do they contain messages that demand (or allow for) decoding on a more socially and politically sophisticated level? Given their themes, examples, and structures, stories such as *O mistério do coelho pensante* and *A mulher que matou os peixes* certainly seem to admit more than one possible interpretation. Lispector's penultimate "children's story," however, seems textually less able to sustain this kind of "politicized" reading and seems closer to what we ordinarily think of as children's literature.[35]

Quase de verdade (1978)

Lispector's final "children's story," *Quase de verdade,* features Lispector's dachshund, Ulisses, as narrator. Ulisses tells the story of a certain fig tree that, unhappy because it is not bearing fruit, becomes consumed by jealousy, envy, and finally a thirst for vengeance. Entering into a conspiracy with a cloud (which is also a witch), the fig tree manages to wreak havoc in the pastoral world around him. Controlling his minions by means of an evil power, the fig tree comes to exert an enslaving force on the other creatures. These other creatures then band together . . . exigir os seus direitos, pôr ovos para eles mesmos, reclamar comida, água, dormida e descanso"[36] (to demand their rights, to lay eggs themselves, to find food, water, rest and sleep). Finally, through the intervention of Oxalá, the other creatures, led by Odissea (a hen) and Ovidio (a rooster), are able to break the evil spell and return their world to normal. The fig tree, now repentant, finally bears fruit and all is well once again.

Amusing and morally instructive as a "children's story," *Quase de verdade* may also be read as a kind of political statement. After the creatures demand their *direitos* ("rights"), the narrator speaks of *liberdade* ("Queremos a liberdade de cantar só de dia!"; We want the freedom to sing only during the day!) and the need for "sacrifice" ("às vezes a gente precisa fazer um sacrifício" [16: sometimes people have to make sacrifices]). Later, the narrator speaks of "punishment" for wrongdoing, hunger, slavery, and finally the attainment of freedom.

Just as violence *(A mulher que matou os peixes)* is a real part of the human condition, for children as well as adults, so, too, is the issue of our political identity—what rights we demand for ourselves and others *(Quase de verdade).* Once again, then, we see how Lispector's "children's stories" were written perhaps not only to entertain young people but to instruct them in the sometimes hard but always important lessons about being a member of human society. Applicable to young and old alike, these "children's stories" show Lispector's enduring commitment to telling the truth.

Chapter Five
The Nonfiction Work

Consisting primarily of *crônicas,* newspaper columns, and interviews, Lispector's nonfiction work constitutes a sizable portion of her writing. Always a politically aware person and an "engaged writer," Clarice Lispector kept abreast of the events of her time.[1] In Brazil, for example, during the turbulent 1960s and 1970s, she participated in demonstrations in support of political freedom and artistic expression (see Lispector's interviews with Chico Buarque, *De corpo inteiro*). Lispector's political consciousness rarely appeared in her work, however, at least not in any overt fashion. When it did appear, as in "Brasília" (*Visão do esplendor,* 1975), "Literatura e justiça" (*A legião estrangeira,* 1964), and "Mineirinho" (*A legião estrangeira,* 1964), it was typically tempered with a series of personal revelations about the author herself and how she felt about the world around her. Covering a wide variety of subjects, Lispector's nonfiction prose is stylistically similar to her fiction. There is the same careful attention to words and the thoughts they convey, to the necessity of perceiving the truth of things, and to telling it in a way that reveals as much about the perceiver as the perceived. This latter tendency is particularly apparent in the interviews Lispector did for the magazine *Manchete.* It also appears, though in more oblique ways, in the chronicles Lispector wrote as a columnist for the *Jornal do Brazil* (a paper) and *Fotos e Fatos* (a magazine).

A legião estrangeira (1964)

Composed of both fiction (see chapter 4) and nonfiction (described as *crônicas* or "chronicles"), *A legião estrangeira* offers many valuable insights into Lispector's aesthetic vision. Part 2 of the work, entitled "Fundo de gaveta" (Bottom of the drawer), contains more than twenty-eight narratives, ranging from a single line or two ("O cetro," "A ceia divina," and "Aproximação gradativa") to several pages ("Um homen espanhol" and "A pecadora queimada e os anjos harmoniosos," the latter a work written as a diversion while the author awaited the birth of her first child). The pieces cover, or touch upon, a variety of issues: contemporary social events ("Mineirinho"), travel ("Brasília: cinco dias" and "Berna"), individual and national identity ("Um homen público"), art ("Notas sobre dança indu"), and humor ("A posteridade nos julgará").

One of the most salient features of the "Fundo de gaveta" section of *A legião estrangeira,* however, is the number of pieces that deal directly with Lispector's own art of fiction. The following pieces can be found in English translation in *Review 24,* (37–43, trans. G. Pontiero):[2] "Já que se há de escrever" ("Since One Feels Obliged to Write"), "A pesca milagrosa" ("Miraculous Fishing"), "Lembrar-se" ("Evocation"), "Aventura" ("Adventure"), and "O segrêdo" ("The Secret"). All these speak in general terms about how Lispector understands the act of writing and the nature of words. "A explicação inútil" (Some useless explanation), on the other hand, speaks directly about the details surrounding the creation of the stories included in *Laços de família*; three other pieces, "Escrever, prolongar o tempo" (Writing and prolonging time), "Dois modos" (Two ways), and "Escrevendo" (Writing), offer fascinating and useful insights into Lispector's very personal creative process. From "Dois modos," for example, we learn: "when writing I have insights that are 'passive' and so intimate that they write themselves the very instant I perceive them without the intervention of any so-called thought processes. For this reason, I make no choice when writing."[3] And in "Escrevendo," Lispector declares, "I am incapable of 'drafting' a manuscript. I am incapable of 'relating' an idea or of 'dressing up an idea' with words. What comes to the surface, is already expressed in words or simply fails to exist. Upon writing the text, there is always the certainty (seemingly paradoxical) that what confuses the writer is the necessity of using words. This is the real trouble."[4]

A legião estrangeira, then, is an intriguing book for the reader interested in reading some of Lispector's best short fiction and in reading some of her own comments about it. As such, it is a work of singular importance in the Lispectorian canon.

Visão do esplendor: impressões leves (1975)

Like the nonfiction of *A legião estrangeira,* the chronicles of *Visão do esplendor* differ widely in terms of their subject matter. Some of these pieces, such as "Contraveneno," are archly funny, while others, such as "Vergonha de viver," manage to be both autobiographically revealing and gently ironic at the same time. "Vergonha de viver," for example, relates some amusing anecdotes about Lispector's childhood in Recife and her adolescent years in Rio. She comments briefly on some of the early stories that she wrote and sent to a paper hoping to see them published (none ever was), and on her three-act, four-page-long play about "love." She notes that she hid the work behind a bookcase until one day, fearing that someone would find it and "reveal her," she tore it up. Lispector ends this essay by noting that she wishes she had not destroyed the play because she wonders what, as a nine-year-old girl, she thought about love.

Another, longer piece is "Brasília," the first section of which had appeared earlier in *A legião estrangeira*. Lispector attended a conference in Brasília in 1974 and this experience led her to expand upon her earlier comments (published in *ALE*), which were written in 1962.

There is a political note to the entire essay. In the first (1962) part, for example, we read, "A construção de Brasília: a de um Estado totalitário"[5] (The construction of Brasília: that of a totalitarian State). The issue of "totalitarianism" is not carried any further, however, though certain political aspects of the city and its inhabitants are. Lispector asks, for example, if (in part 2, i.e., 1974) there was much crime in the city. She is told that in the neighborhood, or district, of Grama there were about three homicides per week (14).

Lispector's tendency in the second part of her essay to describe Brasília categorically, but to do so using the vehicle of metaphors. She says, at one point, "Brasília é ferrinho de dentista" (26: Brasília is a dentist's tool). She later notes, "Brasília é Lei Física" (30: Brasília is a Law of Physics) and "Brasília é esplendor" (33: Brasília is splendor).

In general terms, the techniques employed in "Brasília" are typical and fully representative of what Lispector does in the other forty-four pieces. Many of these other narratives, including "Cisne," "Domingo de tarde," and "O erro dos inteligentes," are so short and cryptic that they are more like impressionistic fragments of thought than formal essays or the popular Brazilian *crônica* or "chronicle." Here Lispector gives the reader a deeply personal interpretation of and response to a specific locale—the federal capital of Brasília. In reading about the city, however, the reader also begins to learn about Clarice Lispector herself. As Lispector is affected by and responds to the city, the reader discovers the thoughts and feelings that this experience engenders in the author. Lispector's reportage of this reactive process parallels the experiential process undergone by the characters in her fiction. What "happens" in the two modes of expression (her fiction and nonfiction) is basically the same; Lispector's characters do not "act" nearly as much as they react, psychologically and physiologically, to what is happening around them. Thus Lispector's reaction to Brasília is intensely subjective, so much so that at times its expression becomes paradoxical, ironic, and heavily metaphoric. This, basically, is what takes place in Lispector's fiction as well.

Finally, it is interesting to note that in *Visão do esplendor,* published in 1975, Lispector felt compelled to try to explain her understanding of what her novels were "about." In "O 'verdadeiro' romance" (The "True" novel) she says that she finds the "true novel" boring. She says, too, that she does not write this kind of novel, that when she writes she is guided by a sense of search and discovery.[6] Becoming specific, she notes that as a fiction writer she does not think about syntax (that most unusual aspect of her style) per se but in terms of its being the linguistic function that best enables her to enter into and be affected by the ideas that she has in mind while she is performing the act of writing (103). She also comments on her sense of how "objects" affect her thinking (and her characters' thinking) and about why she thinks *sofisma* ("sophistry" or "fraud") came to be regarded by her as one of her defects (104–5).

An essay of a similarly literary nature is "O primeiro livro de cada uma de minhas vidas" (The first book of each of my lives), which discusses some of the books and authors prized by Lispector at different times in her early years. Among her favorites are *Reinações de Narizinho,* by Monteiro Lobato (see "Felicidade clandestina," a story perhaps autobiographical in essence); *O lobo da estepe,* by Hermann Hesse (*Steppenwolf;* Lispector notes here how, in fact, Hesse did have a direct influence on her early writings, how she was especially struck by his treatment of the "interior journey," and how she began to write a long story imitating Hesse's treatment of this theme); and finally a book of stories by Katherine Mansfield, with whom Lispector felt an immediate and powerful kinship (117–19).[7]

If nothing else, Lispector's diverse nonfiction should dispel the notion that she was an excessively "precious" writer, an aesthete who lived apart from the struggles of her fellow citizens. In fact, nothing could be farther from the truth. Clarice Lispector was a highly refined writer, but she was also a politically aware human being. In particular, she was a highly intelligent, well-educated, and well-read woman who was quite cognizant of the human condition. Indeed, insofar as the "human condition" can be said to relate to problems of communication between human beings, this was, in a sense, the essential theme of her work, the fiction as well as the nonfiction.

De corpo inteiro (1975)

Published the same year as *Visão do esplendor, De corpo inteiro* is not a collection of chronicles but a collection of the interviews Lispector did for the magazine *Manchete*. These interviews, like the chronicles, cover a wide range of people. Many writers are interviewed, as are musicians (Chico Buarque), folklorists (Djanira), architects (Oscar Niemeyer), bureaucrats (Minister of Planning Reis Velloso), physicists (Mário Schemberg), literary critics (Benedito Nunes; Nunes is one of the most comprehensive authorities on Clarice Lispector's work), and psychiatrists (Dr. J. D. Azulay).

More even than in the case of Lispector's chronicles, these interviews teach us almost as much about Clarice Lispector and her work as they do about the person who is the object of the interview. This is not surprising when Lispector is talking with another writer—for example, Jorge Amado, Érico Veríssimo, Vinícius de Morais, Dinah Silveira de Queiróz, or Nélida Piñon—but it is a little startling when she is talking with the diplomat and sculptor Maria Martins, the musician Jacques Klein, or the actress Tônia Carrero.

In several of these interviews, such as those with Oscar Niemeyer, Chico Buarque, and Tom Jobim, Lispector's political dimension surfaces. Bringing up the matter of student demonstrations in the interview with Chico Buarque (Buarque himself being a politically aware entertainer), Lispector asks him his opinion of student activism in Brazil and elsewhere. Buarque responds at length, but ends by reminding Lispector that he had seen her marching in some of those same demonstrations and by asking her what her motives had been. Lispector responds by saying that she marched for the same reasons Buarque had, but then she abruptly changes the subject.[8]

An interesting characteristic of many of these interviews, and one that also casts additional light on one of Lispector's most essential themes, is that Lispector frequently asks her subjects for their feelings and ideas about love. Typical of her handling of this issue is her interview with Jorge Amado:

C.L.: Você escreve muito sobre o amor. O que é o amor?
(You write a lot about love. What is love?)
J.A.: É a própria vida, e o melhor da vida, tudo.
(It's life itself, the best of life, everything.)
(14)

She asks the same question of several different people, among them Pablo Neruda, Érico Veríssimo, and Hílio Pelegrino. The impression one finally gets, here and in her fiction, is that for Clarice Lispector love is a vital and powerful life-force, one that binds together all human activity but one that can imprison as well as liberate.

Aside from the considerable amount of information that these engaging and enlightening interviews provide us about Clarice Lispector as a woman and an artist, they also show Lispector's erudition, insight, and the synthesizing power of her mind. Lispector's expertise as a journalist is an aspect of her career that has so far received scant attention.[9] For someone interested in eliminating this critical omission, these interviews would be a propitious place to begin.

Para não esquecer (1978)

Published posthumously, *Para não esquecer* is an anthology of some of Lispector's previously published chronicles, essays, and personal reflection. It has 108 selections and no introduction, notes, or other explanatory material.

Chapter Six
Conclusion

At the time of her death in early December 1977, Clarice Lispector was perhaps the most respected writer in Brazil. Never a popular author in the sense that great numbers of people ever read her works, she was from the beginning of her career in 1944 an important author, one whose achievements had already attracted a discerning international audience as well as a national one.

As a Brazilian writer, Lispector will be best remembered for having opened new roads for Brazilian narrative, for having helped (along with Guimarães Rosa) to lead it away from the fertile but ultimately limiting kind of regionalism that had dominated the literary scene in Brazil for several generations. Lispector's first novel, *Perto do coração selvagem,* broke dramatically with this deeply rooted tradition and established a new set of criteria that would help internationalize Brazilian literature and end its cultural and linguistic isolation.

Although many critics find her stories superior to her novels, a critical disposition that undoubtedly owes much to the striking dramatic intensity that characterizes her fiction and that is especially notable in her shorter pieces, there can be no doubt that Lispector was a major precursor of the justly famous "new novel" in Latin America. While not so nearly well known as her Spanish American contemporaries Gabriel García Márquez, Julio Cortázar, José Donoso, and Carlos Fuentes, Clarice Lispector had begun to renovate the novel form in Latin America as early as 1942, when she first began piecing together the strands of the story that would ultimately become her first novel, *Perto do coração selvagem.*

The storm center of that fledgling novel, and a character who, in her visceral verisimilitude and psychic complexity, can be taken as the prototype for later Lispectorian protagonists, was a young woman, the first of a series of memorable female characters Lispector would create. Running the gamut from timid and dependent Ermelinda *(A maçã no escuro),* to the bourgeoise Hausfrau, Ana ("Amor"), to the hopelessly crippled refugee, Macabéa *(A hora da estrela),* to the free but anguished voice of *Um sopro de vida,* Lispector's characters all relate in one fashion or another to the real issues of feminism, self-realization, courage, freedom, and love. It is demeaning to speak of "women writers," so to say that Clarice Lispector has been the most important woman writer in Latin American literature since Sor Juana Inés de la Cruz (1651–1695) is to give Lispector a distinction of dubious value even though it is almost certainly true. Suffice it to say that Clarice Lispector was one of the most original and challenging fiction writers Latin America has seen in the second half of the twentieth century, a writer whose work has yet to receive the critical attention it deserves.

After nine novels, six collections of stories, four "children's books," translation work, interviews, and an abundance of nonfiction pieces, it can be said that Lispector's literary reputation rests solidly on three issues, all of which, seen in the perspective of the early days of her career, were positive and invigorating for Latin American narrative: (1) her style, lyrical and relying on imagery, rhythmical patternings, and metaphoric renderings to convey her basically philosophic subject matter; (2) her structures, built typically around various forms of the epiphany, the interior monologue and the fluid presentation of a character's quicksilver psychic state; and (3) her themes, reflecting the anxieties, the isolation, and the urge toward self-awareness that characterize modern men and women.

A writer of a highly refined, often rarefied poetic prose, yet a writer also possessed of a strong and humanitarian social conscience, Clarice Lispector was one of Latin America's most singular voices in the turbulent post–World War II era. One of modern Latin America's most powerful narrativists, her work will endure.

Notes and References

Chapter One

1. S. Y. Campedelli and B. Abdala, Jr., eds., *Clarice Lispector* (São Paulo, 1981), 3.
2. Luís Costa Lima, "A desarticulação da realidade," *A literatura no Brasil*, ed. Afrânio Coutinho (Rio de Janeiro: Editorial Sul Americana, 1970), 5:461. An English translation of the citation appears in *Modern Latin American Literature*, eds. David William and Virginia Ramos Foster (New York: Frederick Ungar, 1975), 1:488.
3. Elizabeth Lowe, "The Passion According to C. L.," (an interview with Clarice Lispector), in *Review 24* (New York: The Center for Inter-American Relations, 1979), 37.
4. "Vergonha de viver," in *Visão do esplendor* (Rio de Janeiro: Livraria Francisco Alves, 1975), 75–77.
5. Campedelli and Abdala, *Clarice Lispector*, 4.
6. Ibid. In "O primeiro livro de cada de minhas vidas" *(Visão do esplendor)* Lispector discusses the impact these early influences had on her.
7. Ibid.
8. Bella Jozef, "Chronology: Clarice Lispector," trans. Elizabeth Lowe, in *Review 24*, 25.
9. Jozef, "Chronology: Clarice Lispector," 25.
10. Campedelli and Abdala, *Clarice Lispector*, 4.
11. Ibid.
12. Lowe, "The Passion According to C. L.," 36.
13. Ibid.
14. Renard Perez, *Escritores brasileiros contemporâneos*, 2d ser. (Rio de Janeiro, 1971), 73.
15. Ibid.
16. Ibid.
17. Clarice Lispector, "Adventure," trans. Giovanni Pontiero, in *Review 24*, 39.
18. Campedelli and Abdala, *Clarice Lispector*, 5.
19. Jozef, "Chronology: Clarice Lispector," 25.
20. Ibid.

21. Gregory Rabassa, trans. *The Apple in the Dark* (New York, 1967), 11.

22. Ralph Freedman, *The Lyrical Novel: Studies in Hermann Hesse, André Gide and Virginia Woolf* (Princeton: Princeton University Press, 1963), 76–94.

23. Rabassa, introduction to *The Apple in the Dark*, xii.

24. Freedman, *The Lyrical Novel*, 1–41.

25. Perez, *Escritores brasileiros contemporâneos*, 76 (translation by Earl E. Fitz).

26. Rabassa, introduction to *The Apple in the Dark*, xii.

27. "The Foreign Legion," trans. Giovanni Pontiero, in *Review 24*, 37–43.

28. Emir Rodríguez Monegal, "The Contemporary Brazilian Novel," in *Fiction in Several Languages*, ed. Henri Peyre (Boston: Beacon Press, 1968), 15.

29. Ibid.

30. J. A. Motta Pesanha, "Itinerário da Paixão," *Cadernos brasileiros* 7, no. 29 (1985). 63–76.

31. For a brief discussion of this issue, see "Era uma vez," *A legião estrangeira* (Rio de Janeiro, 1964), 140.

32. An English translation (by Earl E. Fitz) of this story has been accepted for publication by the *Latin American Literary Review*.

33. Jozef, "Chronology: Clarice Lispector," 26.

34. Lowe, "The Passion According to C. L.," 36.

35. Ibid., 37.

36. An unpublished English translation of this novel has been done by Professor Richard Mazzara and Ms. Lorri Paris, both of Oakland University (Michigan).

37. At the current time there exists an unpublished translation (by Elizabeth Lowe and Earl E. Fitz) of this novel.

38. Jozef, "Chronology: Clarice Lispector," 26.

39. Campedelli and Abdala, *Clarice Lispector*, 6 (translation by Earl E. Fitz).

40. There exists some discrepancy as to the exact date of burial; Bella Jozef writes (*Review 24*, 26) that it was December 11, 1977. Giovanni Pontiero, however, notes in the same volume (37) that Lispector "died of cancer on December 9, 1977. Three days later on her fifty-seventh birthday, she was buried after a simple ceremony."

Chapter Two

1. Lowe, "The Passion According to C. L.," 37.

2. Ibid., 34.

3. For a further discussion of this issue, see Elizabeth Lowe's *The City in Brazilian Literature* (Rutherford, N. J., 1982).

4. Claude Hulet, *Brazilian Literature* (Washington, D. C.: Georgetown University Press, 1975) 3:3.

5. Ibid.

6. Ibid., 3:4.

7. For an excellent study of the "Northeastern Novel," see Fred Ellison's *Brazil's New Novel* (Berkeley: University of California Press, 1954).

8. Hulet, *Brazilian Literature*, 3:8.

9. Ibid.

10. Giovanni Pontiero, "The Drama of Existence in *Laços de família*," *Studies in Short Fiction* 8, no. 1 (Winter 1971):256–66.

11. Motta Pessanha, "Itinerário da Paixão," 63–76.

12. Cândido, *Review 24*, 37.

13. Monegal, "Contemporary Brazilian Novel," 13.

14. Rabassa, introduction to *The Apple in the Dark*, p. xii.

15. Assis Brasil, *Clarice Lispector* (Rio de Janeiro, 1969) 72–73. For an English translation of this citation see *Modern Latin American Literature*, 1:487–88.

16. Monegal, "Contemporary Brazilian Novel," 15.

17. Jozef, "Chronology: Clarice Lispector," 24.

18. Rabassa, introduction to *The Apple in the Dark*, xii.

19. See R. L. Scott-Buccleuch and Mário Teles de Oliveira, eds., *Anthology of Brazilian Prose* (São Paulo: Editores Ática, 1971), 328.

20. Monegal, "Contemporary Brazilian Novel," 14.

21. Lispector, *A maçã no escuro*, 3d ed. (Rio de Janeiro, 1970), 16.

22. Lowe, "Passion According to C. L.," pp. 34–35. See also Earl E. Fitz, "The Leitmotif of Darkness in Seven Novels by Clarice Lispector," *Chasqui* 7, no. 2 (1979):18–28.

23. Samuel Putnam, *Marvelous Journey: A Survey of Four Centuries of Brazilian Literature* (New York: Alfred A. Knopf, 1948), 137–38.

24. Earl E. Fitz, "Feminist Characterization in the Fiction of Clarice Lispector," *Modern Language Studies* 10, no. 3 (1980):51–61. For a discussion of Lispector's rejection of the term *feminist*, see Maria Luisa Nunes's "Clarice Lispector: Artista andrógina ou escritora?," *Revista Iberoamericana* 50, no. 126 (January-March 1984):281–89.

25. Griselda Gambaro, "Feminism or Femeneity?" *Américas* 30, no. 1 (October 1978):18–19. In his book *On Deconstruction* Jonathan Culler offers an interpretation of "feminist criticism" that can be applied to Lispector's work in a most interesting and thought-provoking fashion.

26. Emir Rodríguez Monegal, *El boom de la novela latinoamericana* (Caracas, 1972), 90–91.

27. Monegal, "Contemporary Brazilian Novel," 16.

28. In conversation, the Graduate Center, City University of New York, 1972.

29. José Donoso, *The Boom in Spanish American Literature: A Personal History*, trans. Gregory Kolovakos (New York: Columbia University and the Center for Inter-American Relations, 1977).

30. Teresinha Alves Pereira, "Coincidencia de la técnica de Julio Cortázar y Clarice Lispector," *Nueva Narrativa Hispanoamericana* 3, no. 1 (January 1973):103–11.

31. Earl E. Fitz, "The Rise of the New Novel in Latin America: A Lyrical Aesthetic," *Inter-Muse* 2, (1979):17–27.

32. Rabassa, introduction to *The Apple in the Dark*, x.

33. David Gallagher, *Modern Latin American Literature* (London: Oxford University Press, 1973), 91–92.

34. E. R. Monegal was one of the first to do so. See his "Contemporary Brazilian Novel," 16–18.

35. Although many commentators have noted the similarities that appear to exist between Lispector's use of this word and the ways the existentialists use it, Lispector herself has stated categorically that her "nausea" is not that of Jean-Paul Sartre. See *Review 24*, 36.

36. Lispector, *The Passion According to G. H.*, translated by Jack Tomlins, in *The Borzoi Anthology of Latin American Literature*, eds. Emir Rodríguez Monegal and Thomas Colchie (New York, 1977), 2:780–81.

37. Rabassa, introduction to *The Apple in the Dark*, xiv.

38. Lispector, *The Apple in the Dark*, trans. Gregory Rabassa (New York, 1967), 94–98.

39. Colin Wilson, *Introduction to the New Existentialism* (Boston: Houghton Mifflin, 1966), 39–41.

40. Monegal, "Contemporary Brazilian Novel," 16.

41. Ibid., 15.

Chapter Three

1. Alceu Amoroso Lima, from the dust jacket of *A cidade sitiada*, 3d ed. (Rio de Janeiro: Instituto Nacional do Livro, 1971).

2. For some revealing comments by Lispector herself on this issue, see "O 'verdadeiro' romance" and "o primeiro livro de cada uma de minhas vidas," both from *A visão do esplendor*. See also "Excerpts from the Chronicles of the *Foreign Legion*," trans. G. Pontiero, *Review 24*, 37–43.

3. See "O 'verdadeiro' romance," *A visão de esplendor*, 103–5. As this essay shows, Lispector's own sense of the importance of syntax in her work is very illuminating of her creative process.

4. See Ihab Hassan, "POSTmodernISM," *New Literary History* 3 (1971):5–30 and "The Literature of Silence," in *Innovations*, 93–108.

Benedito Nunes has also written about this important Postmodernist aspect of Lispector's work. See *O mundo de Clarice Lispector,* 63–77.

5. See Maria Luisa Nunes, "Narrative Modes in Clarice Lispector's *Laços de família:* The Rendering of Consciousness," *Luso-Brazilian Review* 14, no. 2 (Winter 1977):174–84.

6. Freedman, *The Lyrical Novel,* 1–17.

7. Álvaro Lins, *Os mortos de sobrecasaca* (Rio de Janeiro: Editôra Civilização Brasileira, 1963), 189–91.

8. Northrop Frye, *The Well-Tempered Critic* (Bloomington: Indiana University Press, 1963).

9. Rabassa, introduction to *The Apple in the Dark,* xii.

10. Monegal, "Contemporary Brazilian Novel," 16.

11. Lispector, *Água viva,* 36–37.

12. Cleanth Brooks, *The Well Wrought Urn: Studies in the Structure of Poetry* (New York: Harcourt, Brace & Co., 1947).

13. Freedman, *The Lyrical Novel,* 1–17.

14. Sharon Spencer, *Space, Time and Structure in the Modern Novel* (New York: New York University Press, 1971), 174.

15. Spencer, *Space, Time and Structure,* 174–75.

16. F. G. Reis, "Quem tem mêdo de Clarice Lispector," *Revista Civilização Brasileira,* no. 17 (January and February 1968):225–34.

17. Adonias Filho, *Modernos ficcionistas brasileiros,* 2d ser. (Rio de Janeiro, 1958), 81.

18. Lins, *Os mortos de sobrecasaca,* 191.

19. Brasil, *Clarice Lispector,* 41.

20. Robert Scholes and Robert Kellogg, *The Nature of Narrative* (New York: Oxford University Press, 1954), 31.

21. Norman Friedman, "Point of View in Fiction: The Development of a Critical Concept," in *The Theory of the Novel,* ed. Philip Stevick (New York: Free Press, 1967), 118.

22. Freedman, *The Lyrical Novel,* 271.

23. Ibid., 272.

24. Ibid., 15.

25. For an interesting discussion of how this process works, see Naomi Lindstrom, "Clarice Lispector: Articulating Women's Experience," *Chasqui* 3, no. 1 (1978):43–52 and "A Discourse Analysis of 'Preciosidade' by Clarice Lispector," *Luso-Brazilian Review* 19, no. 2 (Winter 1982):187–94.

26. Lins, *Os mortos de sobrecasaca,* 191.

27. Two of Lispector's most perceptive critics, Benedito Nunes and Assis Brasil, have written important books focusing on these issues. See Nunes, *O mundo de Clarice Lispector* (Manaus, 1966) and Brasil, *Clarice Lispector.*

28. Massaud Moisés, "Clarice Lispector and Cosmic Vision," trans. Sara M. McCabe, *Studies in Short Fiction* 8, no. 1 (Winter 1971):272.

29. Freedman, *The Lyrical Novel*, 134.

30. George Steiner, *After Babel: Aspects of Language and Translation* (New York: Oxford University Press, 1975), 32, 46, 226, 285, 407, 415. Steiner's comments on "alternity" in language meaning and human discourse are particularly useful in gaining a new perspective on how and why Lispector's characters speak (and think) as they do. A major difference, however, is that Lispector's characters, seeking always to find the "right words," are more confused (like Martim or Joana) than deliberately misleading. The ambiguity of language is what connects the language use of Lispector's characters to Steiner's sense of "alternity."

31. Steiner, *After Babel*, 46.

32. Lowe, "The Passion According to C. L.," 34–35.

33. Scholes and Kellogg, *The Nature of Narrative*, 177–78.

34. Ibid., 177.

35. Freedman, *The Lyrical Novel*, 203.

36. Filho, *Modernos ficcionistas brasileiros*, 82.

Chapter Four

1. *Perto do coração selvagem* (Rio de Janeiro, 1944), 198. Unless otherwise indicated, the English translation of this and other texts is by Earl E. Fitz.

2. Lowe, *City in Brazilian Literature*, 140.

3. Jozef, "La recuperación de la palabra poética," *Revista Iberoamericana* 50, no. 126 (January-March 1984):239–57.

4. Rabassa, introduction to *The Apple in the Dark*, xv.

5. *A paixão segundo G. H.* (Rio de Janeiro, 1964), 216; hereafter page references cited in parentheses in the text.

6. Monegal, "Contemporary Brazilian Novel," 15.

7. *Uma aprendizagem ou o livro dos prazeres* (Rio de Janeiro, 1969), 48.

8. Benedito Nunes, *Leitura de Clarice Lispector* (São Paulo, 1973), 76–77.

9. *Água viva* (Rio de Janeiro, 1973), 97. Translation by Elizabeth Lowe and Earl Fitz; hereafter page references cited in parentheses in the text.

10. Tzvetan Todorov, *The Poetics of Prose,* trans. R. Howard (Ithaca: Cornell University Press, 1977), 80–88.

11. Jozef, "Chronology: Clarice Lispector," 26.

12. Ibid.

13. *A hora da estrela* (Rio de Janeiro, 1977), 100.

14. Earl E. Fitz, "Clarice Lispector's *Um sopro de vida:* The Novel as Confession"; soon to be published by *Hispania.*

15. *Um sopro de vida; pulsações* (Rio de Janeiro, 1978), 11; herefter page references cited in parentheses in the text.

16. In her book *A escritura de Clarice Lispector* (Petrópolis, 1979), Olga de Sá challenges this idea, however, arguing (following Jauss's views) that Lispector's fiction vacillates between a "metaphoric-metaphysical" polarity.

17. *Alguns contos,* 34 (trans. G. Pontiero); hereafter page references cited in parentheses in the text.

18. "Love," in *Family Ties,* trans. Giovanni Pontiero (Austin, 1972), 43; hereafter page references cited in parentheses in the text.

19. Lowe, "The Passion According to C. L.," 36.

20. Rita Herman, "Existence in *Laços de família,*" *Luso-Brazilian Review* 4, no. 1, (June 1967):69–74.

21. "The Foreign Legion," 40.

22. Lowe, "The Passion According to C. L.," 34. Lowe's critical introduction to her interview is an excellent summary of Lispector's major thematic, stylistic, and structural characteristics.

23. "The Buffalo," in *Family Ties,* trans. G. Pontiero, 152.

24. "Viagem a Petrópolis," in *A legião estrangeira* (Rio de Janeiro, 1964), 70.

25. "Sofia's Disasters," trans. Elizabeth Lowe, *Review 24,* 27–33.

26. "Felicidade clandestina," in *Felicidade clandestina* (Rio de Janeiro, 1971), 8.

27. This was when Lispector was "discovered" (according to the Brazilian press covering the event) by Spanish America, referred to as "Latin America" by the Brazilians. See Monegal, "Clarice Lispector en sus Libros y en mi Recuerdo," *Revista Iberoamericana* 50, no. 26 (January-March 1984):234.

28. "Marmosets," trans. Elizabeth Bishop, in *The Eye of the Heart* (New York, 1973), 455–57.

29. "Macacos," in *Felicidade clandestina,* 95.

30. For a succinct statement about how theme and technique merge in Lispector's fiction, see Giovanni Pontiero, "Excerpts from *The Foreign Legion,*" in *Review 24,* 37–43. Page 38 is of particular relevance here, however.

31. This is another aspect of Lispector's work that has been largely ignored by the critics. For Lispector, the act of writing was preeminently an erotic experience, one that is at first solitary (the writer) but that quickly converts itself (through the reader and the act of reading) into a universal eroticism. See Monegal, "Clarice Lispector en sus libros y en mi recuerdo," 237.

32. *O mistério do coelho pensante* (Rio de Janeiro, 1967), 4; hereafter page references cited in parentheses in the text.

33. Lispector was always very conscious of how the reader of her work was required to "read between the lines." For more critical commentary on this feature of her work, see Olga de Sá, "Clarice Lispector: Processos Criativos," *Revista Iberoamericana,* 50, no. 126 (January-March 1984):259–280, esp. 259–60.

34. Professor Frederick C. H. Garcia has argued that *A vida íntima de Laura* is the most successful of Lispector's children's stories and that it, along with Lispector's final adult works, reflects a growing reembracing of plot, a plot system that is basically traditional and mimetic in nature. See "Os Livros infantis de Clarice Lispector," *Minas Gerais Suplemento Literário,* 10 February 1979, 4–5.

35. Though not a "children's story" per se, the tale "Uma história de tanto amor" (A story of a great love), from *Felicidade clandestina,* offers a revealing comparative contrast for readers interested in seeing how differently Lispector can deal with children and with the themes (love, hate, violence, death, identity, and even cannibalism, for example) that ostensibly appear in their literature.

36. Lispector, *Quase de verdade* (Rio de Janeiro, 1968), 14; hereafter page references cited in parentheses in the text.

Chapter Five

1. For Lispector's own discussion of this key issue see "Literatura e justiça" (Literature and justice), in *Seleta de Clarice Lispector,* ed. R. C. Gomes and A. G. Hill (Brasília, 1975), xiii. Lispector herself declares, in response to a question about her "political awareness," "Na verdade sinto-me engajada. Tudo o que escrevo está ligado, pelo menos dentro de mim, à realidade em que vivemos" (xiii: "In truth, I feel myself 'engaged.' Everything I write is connected, at least inside of me, to the reality in which we live").

2. Giovanni Pontiero's introduction to his translation of selected segments from *The Foreign Legion (A legião estrangeira)* offers the reader a very useful overview of Lispector's life and work. Another source of illuminating and revealing information about how Lispector went about the writing of her fiction can be found in "Que mistérios tem Clarice?," in *Seleta de Clarice Lispector,* viii–xiv.

3. "The Foreign Legion," 41.

4. Ibid., 43.

5. Lispector, *Visão do esplendor* (Rio de Janeiro, 1975), 10; hereafter page references cited in parentheses in the text.

6. This self-effacing concept is reiterated in another statement Lispector once made about how "intellectual" she is: "I know very little. Yet

this lack of knowledge acts to my advantage—like virgin territory, my mind is free of preconceptions. My lack of knowledge is my *largesse* and preserves what is best in me. By knowing little, I shall come to understand everything. The limitations of my knowledge constitute my truth" ("The Foreign Legion," 38).

7. The here acknowledged influence these two writers had on Lispector's early development tends to substantiate my basic conviction, argued here and elsewhere, that Lispector's fiction was always fundamentally lyrical (see Freedman's *Lyrical Novel*) in theme, structure, and style and that it lends itself to a critical approach from this perspective.

8. Lispector, *De corpo inteiro* (Rio de Janeiro, 1975), 69; hereafter page references cited in parentheses in the text.

9. One of the very few existing commentaries done on this important but almost wholly overlooked aspect of Lispector's work is the short piece by Alberto Dines that functions as a kind of introduction to *De corpo inteiro* (Rio de Janeiro: Editôra Artenova, 1975).

Selected Bibliography

PRIMARY SOURCES

1. Novels
Perto do coração selvagem. Rio de Janeiro: A Noite, 1944.
O lustre. Rio de Janeiro: Editôra Asir, 1946.
A cidade sitiada. Rio de Janeiro: A Noite, 1949.
A maçã no escuro. Rio de Janeiro: Francisco Alves, 1961.
A paixão segundo G. H. Rio de Janeiro: Editôra do Autor, 1964.
Uma aprendizagem ou o livro dos prazeres. Rio de Janeiro: Editôra Sabiá, 1969.
Água viva. Rio de Janeiro: Artenova, 1973.
A hora da estrela. Rio de Janeiro: José Olympio, 1977.
Um sopro de vida: pulsações. Rio de Janeiro: Nova Fronteira, 1978.

2. Stories
Alguns contos. Rio de Janeiro: Ministério de Educação e Saúde, 1952.
Laços de família. Rio de Janeiro: Francisco Alves, 1960.
A legião estrangeira. Rio de Janeiro: Editôra do Autor, 1964.
Felicidade clandestina. Rio de Janeiro: Sabiá, 1971.
A imitação da rosa. A collection of previously published stories. Rio de Janeiro: Editôra Artenova, 1973.
Onde estivestes de noite. Rio de Janeiro: Artenova, 1974.
A via crucis do corpo. Rio de Janeiro: Artenova, 1974.
A bela e a fera. Rio de Janeiro: Nova Fronteira, 1979.

3. Children's literature
O mistério do coelho pensante. Rio de Janeiro: José Álvaro, 1967.
A mulher que matou os peixes. Rio de Janeiro: Sabiá, 1968.
A vida íntima de Laura. Rio de Janeiro: José Olympio, 1974.
Quase de verdade. Rio de Janeiro: Editôra Rocco, 1978.

4. Translations by Clarice Lispector
O retrato de Dorian Gray (her Portuguese translation of Oscar Wilde's *The Picture of Dorian Gray*). Rio de Janeiro: Edições de Ouro, 1974.

5. Translations of works by Clarice Lispector:
   novels, portions of novels, and short-story anthologies

Água viva.
   White Water. Translated by Elizabeth Lowe and Earl Fitz; as yet unpublished.
Laços de família.
   Family Ties. Translated by Giovanni Pontiero. Austin: University of Texas, 1972.
A legião estrangeira.
   The Foreign Legion. Translated by Giovanni Pontiero. In *Review 24,* 37–43. New York: Center for Inter-American Relations, 1979.
A maçã no escuro.
   The Apple in the Dark. Translated by Gregory Rabassa. New York: Alfred A. Knopf, 1967.
A mulher que matou os peixes.
   The Woman Who Killed the Fish. Translated by Earl E. Fitz and scheduled to appear in a forthcoming issue of the *Latin American Literary Review.*
A paixão segundo G. H.
   The Passion According to G. H. A portion of the novel translated by Jack E. Tomlins. In *The Borzoi Anthology of Latin American Literature.* New York: Knopf, 1977.

6. Stories translated and published separately
"Better Than to Burn." Translated by Alexis Levitin. In *Latin American Literature Today.* Edited by Anne Fremantle. New York: New American Library, 1977.
"The Man Who Appeared." Translated by Alexis Levitin. In *Latin American Literature Today.* Edited by Anne Fremantle. New York: New American Library, 1977.
"Marmosets." Translated by Elizabeth Bishop. In *The Eye of the Heart.* New York: Bard/Avon, 1973.
"Pig Latin." Translated by Alexis Levitin. *Ms.* 13, no. 1 (July 1984):68–69.
"Sofia's Disasters." Translated by Elizabeth Lowe. *Review 24.* New York: The Center for Inter-American Relations, June 1979.
"The Smallest Woman in the World." Translated by Elizabeth Bishop. In *The Eye of the Heart.* New York: Bard/Avon, 1973.
"The Solution." Translated by Elizabeth Lowe. *Fiction* 3 (Winter 1974):24.
"Temptation." Translated by Elizabeth Lowe. *Inter-Muse* 1, no. 1 (1976). Michigan State University.

7. Selected and collected writings
A imitação da rosa. A collection of what were then considered to be Lispector's best stories. Rio de Janeiro: Artenova, 1973.

Para não esquecer. A selection of some of Lispector's chronicles and essays. São Paulo: Ática, 1978.

Seleta de Clarice Lispector. Edited by R. C. Gomes and A. G. Hill. Brasília: Instituto Nacional do Livro, 1975. Selections from the stories and novels are grouped thematically. Each selection is followed by a short critical commentary. Includes a statement by Lispector herself about how and why she wrote, and general critical observations by both Gomes and Hill concerning Lispector's fiction. Very useful.

SECONDARY SOURCES

1. Bibliographies

Fitz, Earl E. "Uma bibliografia de e sôbre Clarice Lispector." *Revista Iberoamericana* 50, no. 126 (January-March 1984):293–304. Includes articles, books, parts of books, book reviews, and newspaper articles published through 1984. Not annotated.

2. Books

Borelli, Olga. *Clarice Lispector: um esboço para um possível retrato.* Rio de Janeiro: Nova Fronteira, 1981. An intimate friend's assessment of how and why Lispector wrote as she did. Contains many statements by Lispector about how she viewed her work. Selected examples of Lispector's work illustrate the many aspects of her fiction.

Brasil, Assis. *Clarice Lispector.* Rio de Janeiro: Editôra Organização Simões, 1969. One of the major critical works on Lispector's fiction; discusses Lispector's place in Brazilian literature and the renovating importance of her stories and performs an intrinsic analysis of her novels through *A paixão segundo G. H.* Also comments on her sense of dramatic structuring and on the characteristics of her technique, style, and process of characterization. Brasil also examines Lispector's philosophical base, citing her mysticism and the existential ethos that pervades her work. Stresses her tendency to use poetic images to move her plots along and cites at length what the critic Álvaro Lins thought about her first novel, *Perto do coração selvagem.*

Campedelli, S. Y., and Abdala, B., Jr. *Clarice Lispector.* São Paulo: Literatura Comentada, 1981. Useful because it offers an overview of Lispector's work and life. Also asks critical questions about specific aspects of her techniques. Includes excerpts of her work and critical explanations of their salient qualities. Meant for a non-expert reader who is coming to Lispector for the first time. Contains biographical information.

Nunes, Benedito. *O mundo de Clarice Lispector.* Manaus: Edições Governo do Estado do Amazonas, 1966. Another of the major critical studies on Lispector's work. Deals with her novels through *A paixão segundo G. H.* and with the basic form and structure of her stories. Focuses closely on the philosophic and linguistic underpinnings of Lispector's fiction. Also contains an informative chapter on the nature of Lispector's characters through *A paixão segundo G. H.*, the "mystical experience" of G. H., and the existential angst and nausea that permeate Lispector's fiction. Also has an important chapter on "absurdity" as it enters into Lispector's fictive world.

————. *Leitura de Clarice Lispector.* São Paulo: Editôra Quirón, 1973. Another prime critical study; offers sensitive and detailed intrinsic discussions of various aspects of Lispector's novels (through *Uma aprendizagem*) and selected stories. Offers clear discussions of technical issues and features excellent use of textual examples. Reviews the philosophic and linguistic foundations of Lispector's prose, and shows why "silence" is so prominent in her work. Has a short but selective bibliography.

Pereira, Teresinha Alves. *Estudo sôbre Clarice Lispector.* Coimbra: Edições Nova Era, 1975. A short critical study that offers several contrasting critical opinions about Lispector's work. Discusses Lispector's place in the history of Brazilian literature and comments briefly on her basic themes and techniques. Focuses on *A maçã no escuro.* Includes evidence of Lispector's critical reception.

Sá, Olga de. *A escritura de Clarice Lispector.* Petrópolis: Vozes, 1979. Applies Jauss's theory of reception to Lispector's fiction. Challenges the nature and function of the epiphany in Lispector's work and argues for a view of her narratives as vacillating between a "metaphoric-metaphysical" polarity. Relies on Peirce's linguistic studies. Thought-provoking preface by Haroldo de Campos.

3. Parts of books

Amora, Antônio Soares. *História da literatura brasileira.* 7th ed., 163–74. São Paulo: Edição Saraiva, 1968. General presentation of post–World War II literature in Brazil and how Lispector fits into its development. Offers a brief view of Lispector in contrast to other writers of her time, such as Guimarães Rosa.

Cândido, Antônio. "No raiar de Clarice Lispector." In *Vários escritos,* 125–31. São Paulo: Livraria Duas Cidades, 1970. Written in 1943 (when Lispector was as yet an unknown writer), this is a short but perceptive assessment of Lispector's first novel, *Perto do coração selvagem.* Cândido notes how silence, lyricism, time, language, and philosophical preoccupations all figure centrally in Lispector's first work. He speaks in

some detail of *Perto do coração selvagem,* for example, about how the
chapter entitled "O Banho" (The bath) can be considered the key
chapter in the reader's understanding of Joana, the protagonist. Also
notes how the structure of the novel is closely linked to the development of its protagonist, Joana.

Castro, Sílvio. *A revolução de palavra,* 263–67. Petrópolis: Editôra Vozes,
1976. Important formalist discussion of Lispector's fiction; argues
that her structurally innovative work derives from her multiple methods of portraiture in regard to her characters, especially their moments
of "revelation." Also discusses Lispector's skill at establishing a "psychological montage" by means of which the changing psychic states
of her characters can be depicted.

Coutinho, Afrânio. *An Introduction to Literature in Brazil.* Translated by
Gregory Rabassa, 249. New York: Columbia University Press, 1960.
The noted Brazilian critic places Lispector in the historical devel-
opment of Brazilian literature and evaluates her contribution to it.
Mentions specifically her "atmospheric" fiction, its "strong emotional
content," and her skill at creating a "metaphorical language."

————. *A literatura no Brasil.* 2d ed., vol. 5 (Modernismo), 449–72.
Perceptive discussion of *Perto do coração selvagem, O lustre, A cidade
sitiada, A maçã no escuro,* and *Laços de família* by one of Brazil's leading
critics. Acknowledges Lispector's "poetic" bent and her singular concern with the relationships among language, cognition, and reality.
Notes parallels between Martim (of *A maçã no escuro*) and Guimarães
Rosa's Riobaldo (of *Grande sertão: veredas*). Also suggests that because
of her themes and techniques Lispector's stories are superior to her
novels. Stresses the originality of her talent.

Filho, Adonias. *Modernos ficcionistas brasileiros.* 2d ser., 81–83. Rio de
Janeiro: Edições Tempo Brasileiro, 1965. Focuses primarily on the
basic characters and themes inherent in Lispector's short stories, which,
says Filho, constitute Lispector's best work. Notes how the monologue
plays a central role in the process of characterization.

Jozef, Bella. *O jogo mágico,* 32–40, 75, 122. Rio de Janeiro: Livraria José
Olympio, 1980. A critical study that focuses on various aspects of
Lispector's narrative technique. Jozef centers her discussion on the
several ways Lispector entwines language with different modes of
existence, especially our consciousness of our own varying levels of
psychic existence. Argues that Lispector's narratives number among
the most "renovative" in all of Latin America. Shows how her basic
structural motif is the moment of self-realization, one typically caused
by some usually trivial external event. In the second part of the article
Jozef discusses *Um sopro de vida* and suggests that it is Lispector's

"definitive" work, the one that most clearly expresses her ideas about the vital link between art and human existence.

Lins, Ávaro. *Os mortos de sobrecasaca,* 186–93. Rio de Janeiro: Editôra Civilização Brasileira, 1963. A study of major importance as regards Lispector's sense of characterization, style, and narrative structuring. Surveys *Perto do coração selvagem,* which Lins praises for its original depiction of a private and psychological "reality," and *O lustre,* which, says Lins, has two notable technical aspects: it is brilliant verbally (its linguistic richness and its ambiguity) but all too often this same verbal brilliance degenerates into mere word games, into what Lins calls "words in the air," with no discernible connection to an external reality.

Lowe, Elizabeth. *The City in Brazilian Literature.* Rutherford: Farleigh Dickinson University Press, 1982. An important discussion of Lispector as a distinctly urban writer. Focuses in particular on *A cidade sitiada, A paixão segundo G. H.,* and *Água viva.* Shows how these novels fit into a general pattern of urban literature in Brazil.

Moisés, Massaud. "Clarice Lispector Contista." In *Temas brasileiros,* 119–24. São Paulo: Conselho Estadual de Cultura, 1964. A short but succinct discussion of Lispector the short-story writer. Notes how radically different were the form and tone of *Laços de família* when it appeared in 1960. Comments on the privately dramatic existences "outlined" (as opposed to "developed") in its stories. Makes some interesting comparative comments about the differences and similarities that exist between Lispector's novels and stories. Calls her style both "poetic" and "surrealist," and is reminded of some of Irene Lisboa's work.

Monegal, Emir Rodríguez. *El boom de la novela latinoamericana,* 27 and 93. Caracas: Editoria Tiempo Nuevo, 1972. Though focusing primarily on the development of the Spanish American "New Novel," Monegal makes an important comparative point in saying that Lispector, along with Guimarães Rosa, ranks as one of the major renovators of the novel form in Latin America. Offers no textual analysis of Lispector's work, but does cite *A paixão segundo G. H.* as an outstanding example of her originality.

———. *The Borzoi Anthology of Latin American Literature,* 779–92. New York: Alfred A. Knopf, 1977. Offers a short but interesting introduction to Lispector, her life and works. Places her in a Latin American perspective, rather than purely as a Brazilian writer. Says that *A paixão segundo G. H.* (a portion of which is translated into English by Jack Tomlins) is one of the most powerful novels of its time.

———. "The Contemporary Brazilian Novel." In *Fiction in Several Languages.* Edited by Henri Peyre, 1–18. Boston: Houghton Mifflin,

1968. A substantial treatment of the development of the Brazilian novel from modernism to 1968. Shows how Guimarães Rosa and Clarice Lispector were the two major forces that changed both the nature and form of the "new novel" in Brazil. Summarizes the linguistic, philosophic, and thematic originality of *A maçã no escuro* and *A paixão segundo G. H.* and puts Lispector into a Latin American context.

Nunes, Benedito. "O mundo imaginário de Clarice Lispector." In *O dorso do tigre*, 93–139. São Paulo: Editôra Perspectiva, 1969. Nunes, Lispector's most thorough and perceptive critic, here focuses on the major characteristics of Lispector's work up to 1969. Comments on Lispector's basic themes, her unique language, and its relationship to her characters' creation as well as their philosophic dilemmas. A major article on Lispector.

Olinto, Antônio. *A verdade da ficção*, 62, 100, 110, 142, 144, 213–16, 226, 227. Rio de Janeiro: Companhia Brasileira de Artes Gráficas, 1966. Examines *A maçã no escuro* as a symbolist novel and places it, as an example of this subgenre, in the European tradition of such writers as Virginia Woolf, James Joyce, and Hermann Hesse. Also comments on how *A maçã no escuro* figures as an important work in terms of how the Brazilian novel was to develop during the 1960s. No textual analysis.

Patai, Daphne. *Myth and Ideology in Contemporary Brazilian Fiction*. Cranbury, N. J.: Fairleigh Dickinson University Press, 1983. Applies myth criticism to *A paixão segundo G. H.* (among other works by other writers) and finds that the Lispector novel, though mythic in terms of structure and the patterning of its images, retains an ideological and social dimension.

Perez, Renard. *Escritores brasileiros contemporâneos*. 2d ser., 69–80. Rio de Janeiro: Editôra Civilização Brasileira, 1964. Offers some interesting biographical information about Lispector's early years and about her work habits. Useful because it shows the early influences on her intellectual formation and how she viewed herself as a writer. Includes an excerpt from *A maçã no escuro* but offers no textual analysis.

Silverman, Malcolm. *Moderna ficção brasileira*. Translated into Portuguese by João Guilherme Linke, 70–84. Brasília: Civilização Brasileira, 1978. A thorough and accurate (if perhaps too brief) summary of Lispector's technical and stylistic characteristics. Offers useful plot summations of Lispector's novels and identifies stories that are connected in some way, thematic, stylistic or structural, to the novels. Good summary of various critical commentators on Lispector's work. Concludes by arguing that had she lived longer, Lispector would have become more openly "feminist" in orientation.

4. Articles

Araújo, Laís Corrêa de. "Texto/Improviso." *Minas Gerais Suplemento Literário,* no. 392 (March 2, 1974):9. A brief but perceptive commentary on the importance of language, or "textuality," in Lispector's fiction. Focuses especially on *Água viva,* a work that shows Lispector moving into the area of metafiction. This article might be especially useful for someone attempting a structuralist or hermeneutic analysis of Lispector's work. Stresses her obsession with "words" and their semiotic relationship to the creative act of writing fiction, of "improvisation."

Bruno, Haroldo. "A Presença Renovadora de Clarice Lispector." *Minas Gerais Suplemento Literário,* July 14, 1979, pp. 6–7. Focusing on *Água viva,* Bruno discusses the various ways, including questions of theme, style, and structure, that Lispector helped to transform Brazilian narrative. Shows her importance in the development of Brazilian fiction. Argues that *Onde estivestes de noite* possesses unity of both form and thought. Suggests, too, that the theme of love constitutes the basis for all moments of self-awareness in her work.

Bryan, C. D. B. "Afraid to be Afraid." *New York Times Book Review,* September 3, 1967, pp. 22–23. Terming Lispector, ". . . an inspired and, at times, beautiful, writer," Bryan also notes that "her overwriting flaws the novel." Bryan terms Martim, the protagonist of *A maçã no escuro* (the book being reviewed), an "anti-hero" who, in Bryan's opinion, is inferior as a novelistic character to the two women characters in the novel.

Cook, Bruce. "Women in the Web." *Review* 73 (Spring 1973):65–66. Reviewing *Family Ties,* Cook notes Lispector's tendency to focus on the sociopsychological dilemmas of modern urban women. Observes that the prolonged intensity and expression of Lispector's focus are uniquely her own. Comments briefly on some of the stories.

Fitz, Earl E. "Clarice Lispector and the Lyrical Novel: A Re-examination of *A maçã no escuro.*" *Luso-Brazilian Review* 14, no. 2 (Winter 1977):153–60. Discusses *A maçã no escuro* as an example of what Ralph Freedman has described as the lyrical novel, a kind of writing characterized by a shift in focus away from the world of action and event and toward a world of awareness and knowledge. This inner world is depicted in patterns of imagery rather than by action.

————. "Clarice Lispector's *Um sopro de vida:* The Novel as Confession." Soon to be published by *Hispania.*

————. "Freedom and Self-Realization: Feminist Characterization in the Fiction of Clarice Lispector." *Modern Language Studies* 10, no. 3 (1980):51–56. Focuses on the intellectual integrity of Lispector's characters and argues that their "feminism" transcends political issues and calls for the unification of men and women. Says that in Lispector's work this impulse is driven by the human need for self-realization and freedom.

―――. "The Leitmotif of Darkness in Seven Novels by Clarice Lispector." *Chasqui: Revista de Literatura Latinoamericana* 7, no. 2 (February 1978):18–28. Argues that darkness is so pervasive in Lispector's fiction because it is a leitmotif. Says that darkness is portrayed through three different modes: the psychological, the philosophical, and the linguistic.

―――. "The Rise of the New Novel in Latin America: A Lyrical Aesthetic." *Inter-Muse* 2 (1979):17–27. Attempts to place Lispector in the context of the Spanish American "New Novel." Compares her work to that of José Lezama Lima, Juan Carlos Onetti, José Donoso, and Carlos Fuentes. Finds that Lispector compares favorably with these better-known renovators of the Latin American novel. Argues, too, that the "New Novel" in Latin America is characterized by its lyrical structuring and by its phenomenological approach to the problem of how language depicts and creates reality.

―――. "Point of View in Clarice Lispector's *A hora da estrela.*" *Luso-Brazilian Review* 19, no. 2 (Winter 1982):195–208. Discusses Lispector's experiments with metafiction and the self-conscious and fallible narrator. Also notes her attempt to merge her penchant for intensely hermetic fiction with social commentary.

Garcia, Frederick C. H. "Os livros infantis de Clarice Lispector." *Minas Gerais Suplemento Literário,* February 10, 1979, pp. 4–5. Discusses Lispector's four books of "children's literature" and finds that only one of them, *A vida íntima de Laura,* succeeds on its merits as literature. Argues that her "children's books" are an important part of her canon.

Goldman, Richard Franko. "The Apple in the Dark." *Saturday Review,* August 19, 1967, pp. 33, 48. In a book review of the novel, Goldman says that Lispector's fourth novel is a "fascinating and distinguished work." He notes how she eschews plot and the "local color" of regionalistic fiction for the metaphorically rendered inner realm of psychological turmoil. Declares that Lispector's real talent as a writer lies in her ability to handle language and the epistemological problems related to it. Notes the stylistic and thematic affinities with Compton-Burnett and Woolf and also sees possible influences from Kafka, Gertrude Stein and Lewis Carroll.

Hamilton, D. Lee. "Some Recent Brazilian Literature." *Modern Language Journal* 32, no. 7 (November 1948):504–7. A short but useful article focusing on *O lustre,* Lispector's second novel. Gives a good sense of how radically different this novel was at the time of its publication.

Shows how Lispector was beginning to write a kind of fiction that was not in the regionalist mode so popular in Brazil at the time.

Herman, Rita. "Existence in *Laços de família.*" *Luso-Brazilian Review* 4, no. 1 (June 1967):69–71. Convincing argument for the existential nature of human existence as presented in Lispector's most respected book of short stories. Interprets the stories sensitively but with an eye toward the philosophical and psychological foundations of the main characters. Sees and points out parallels with Sartre and Camus.

Howlett, Jacques. "Pour que L'Horreur Devienne Lumière." *Quinzaine Littéraire,* no. 293 (January 1–15, 1979):11–12. Focusing on the French translation of *A paixão segundo G. H.,* Howlett discusses Lispector's penchant for depicting the philosophic and psychological anxieties associated with the process of self-discovery, self-illumination, or self-realization.

Jozef, Bella. "Chronology: Clarice Lispector." Translated by Elizabeth Lowe. *Review 24,* June 1979, pp. 24–26. A chronological outline of Lispector's life and works. Notes some generally distinguishing features of each of Lispector's works. Good introduction.

————. "Clarice Lispector: Um sopro de plenitude." *Minas Gerais Suplemento Literário,* no. 688 (December 8, 1979):4. Calling it Lispector's "definitive" work, Jozef discusses *Um sopro de vida* primarily in terms of its linguistic inventiveness and thematic concern over the vital connection between art and life. Jozef calls *Um sopro de vida* Lispector's attempt at autobiographical self-expression but through the filtering objectivity of art. Comments on Lispector's attempt to draw the reader into the creation of the text itself by means of the interplay between the narrative voice and Ângela Pralini, a character "created" by the point of view voice.

————. "Clarice Lispector: La Recuperación de la palabra poética." *Revista Iberoamericana* 50, no. 126 (January–March 1984):239–57. In a very useful article, Jozef focuses on the unusual ways Lispector utilized language in her fiction. Stresses Lispector's struggle to show how poetically charged language not only reveals unexpected aspects of external reality but how it comes to control and even create that reality. Summarizes Lispector's novels and her most famous book of short stories, *Laços de família.* Another useful feature of this article is the brief commentary (with examples) on Lispector's critical reception.

————. Review of *Onde estivestes de noite. Revista Iberoamericana* 50, no. 126 (January–March 1984):317–18. Citing the hybrid quality of these narratives (both stories and nonfiction), Jozef discusses briefly Lispector's continued mastery of poetically and philosophically charged language. Notes how this collection tends to focus on a search for what is most essential, most fundamental, in the human experience. Provides a useful introduction to this overlooked collection of fiction and nonfiction by Lispector.

————. Review of *Um sopro de vida. Revista Iberoamericana* 50, no. 126 (January–March 1984):314–17. In a comprehensive review article, Jozef calls attention to how Lispector's final novel, organized and published by Lispector's friend Olga Borelli, is a metaphor for the human creature in its transcendent desire to control reality by means of artistic creativity. Terming *Um sopro de vida* Lispector's "definitive" novel, Jozef focuses on how Lispector dwelled on the magical and mysterious act of writing, an act that both describes and creates realities. The mystery of the act of writing is an important and overlooked Postmodernist aspect of Lispector's fiction and this article calls attention to it.

Lindstrom, Naomi. "Clarice Lispector: Articulating Women's Experience." *Chasqui* 8, no. 1 (1978):43–52. Focuses on Lispector as a feminist writer whose unique linguistic structures allow her to break through much of the falsity and triviality that have grown up around the treatment of women characters in modern Western literature. Shows how Lispector's "innovative approach to formal issues of artistic representation" constitutes (along with her ontological concerns) an especially significant part of her fiction. Textual analysis centers on the story "Amor" (Love), from *Laços de família.*

————. "A Discourse Analysis of '*Preciosidade*' by Clarice Lispector." *Luso-Brazilian Review* 19, no. 2 (Winter 1982):187–94. An illuminating application of a major critical approach to one of Lispector's most subtle and ambiguous stories. Underscores the crucial issue of language, both spoken and unspoken, as it functions in Lispector's fiction. Compares her treatment of her character in this story to Beauvoir's *Le Deuxième Sexe* and finds the treatment similar. Explores the links among Lispector's existential ethos, her varied depictions of consciousness, and the "femininity" of her writing. Shows how the girl of the story under consideration reveals herself (and is revealed) through an interplay of verbal and nonverbal "discourse."

Lowe, Elizabeth. "The Passion According to C. L." (Interview with Clarice Lispector.) *Review 24,* June 1979, pp. 34–37. An illuminating and revealing interview with Lispector. The questions touch on Lispector's personal life, social conscience, work habits and view of herself as a writer. Includes a very useful introduction to Lispector. Highly recommended.

Lucas, Fábio. "Aspectos de la ficción brasileña contemporánea." *Nueva Narrativa Latinoamericana* 3, no. 1 (January 1973):113–23. A major Brazilian critic, Lucas cites Lispector as one of Brazil's most important post—World War II writers. Places her in the comparative context of Brazilian literature in general and assesses her special significance, which Lucas finds to be basically "transcendental" in its relationship to mimetic reality.

Martins, Wilson. "O novo romance brasileiro contemporáneo." *Inti*, no. 111 (April 1976):27–36. A critical overview of the state of the Brazilian novel in the 1960s and 1970s. Finds Lispector one of its major renovators. Puts her in perspective as a Brazilian novelist. Useful for scholars interested in the development of the novel as a literary form in Latin America.

Modern Latin American Literature. Edited by David William Foster and Virginia Ramos Foster, 484–91. New York: Frederick Ungar, 1975. Excerpts, translated (when necessary) into English, from selected critical studies of Lispector's work. The critical selections are excellent. Includes references to the full text. Very useful as a first step in any critical approach to Lispector's work.

Moisés, Massaud. "Clarice Lispector: Fiction and Cosmic Vision." Translated by Sara M. McCabe. *Studies in Short Fiction* 8, no. 1 (Winter 1971):268–81. An important study of Lispector's short fiction, especially that of *Laços de família* and the often-neglected *A legião estrangeira*. Finds Lispector a profoundly philosophic writer who concentrates on the nature of human existence but delivers her treatment of it by means of a personal vision that is "cosmic" (or mythic) rather than social or overtly political. Discusses the importance of animals to her work, how her stories "gravitate around a dramatic unity," and her tendency to utilize biblical themes.

Monegal, Emir Rodríguez. "Clarice Lispector en sus libros y en mi recuerdo." *Revista Iberoamericana* 50, no. 126 (January–March 1984):231–38. Offers a personal view of Lispector by one of her most insightful critics. Tells of conversations and dinners he had with Lispector and of what Lispector was like, both as a person and as "La Gran Dama" of Brazilian letters. Discusses briefly her participation in the World Witchcraft Congress, when, according to the Brazilian press, Lispector was "discovered" by the "Latin Americans," as the Brazilians referred to the Spanish Americans. Discusses the "mystery" of the act of writing (a major sub-theme of her work) by comparing Lispector with Borges.

Nunes, Benedito. "Dos narradores brasileños." *Revista de Cultura* 9, no. 29 (December 1969):187–204. Comparing Lispector's work to that of Osman Lins, Nunes, Lispector's most incisive critic, discusses the important Postmodernist quality of silence in Lispector's work, especially in *Perto do coração selvagem, A maçã no escuro,* and *A paixão segundo G. H.* (the three novels he notes). Talks about how in these novels Lispector achieves a union of language and existence and how these two crucial aspects of her fiction recall Wittgenstein's sense of silence in language use, thereby imparting the strong philosophical cast to Lispector's narratives.

Nunes, Maria Luisa. "Narrative Modes in Clarice Lispector's *Laços de família:* The Rendering of Consciousness." *Luso-Brazilian Review* 14, no. 2 (Winter 1977):174–84. Offers a close reading of several of the stories from *Laços de família.* Examines how Lispector's most characteristic feature, her representation of consciousness, derives from her handling of such narrative modes of expression as narrated monologue, interior monologue, internal analysis, and direct discourse. Argues that Lispector relies on several narrative techniques, some traditional and some not, to render her characters' ever-changing levels of awareness.

————. "Clarice Lispector: Artista andrógina ou escritora?" *Revista Iberoamericana* 50, no. 126 (January–March 1984):281–89. Comparing Lispector to Virginia Woolf, Nunes notes the importance that, throughout her fiction, Lispector put on the question of the artist's identity. Nunes also stresses Lispector's penchant for characters whose quests are acts of creation, her importance as a linguistic innovator, and (although she has denied having feminist intentions) her very real concern over the social and psychological problems of women.

Patai, Daphne. "Clarice Lispector and the Clamor of the Ineffable." *Kentucky Romance Quarterly* 27 (1980):133–49. A thought-provoking reading of *A paixão segundo G. H.* that focuses on Lispector's linguistic representation of what is an essentially mystical (and paradoxical) experience; Patai argues, however, that Lispector's narrator, G. H., speaks with a voice characterized by two stylistic features: "a tendency toward grandiose and grandiloquent expressions" and "an affinity for postulary formulations which appear as definitions." Patai believes that these expressions are inconsistent with G. H.'s basically mystical experience and that their frequency "deprives them of any substance and impact." Suggests that here Lispector uses literature for purposes of mystification.

Pereira, Teresinha Alves. "Coincidéncia de la técnica narrativa de Julio Cortázar y Clarice Lispector." *Nueva Narrativa Hispanoamericana* 3, no. 1 (January 1973):103–11. An interesting piece of scholarship showing how both Julio Cortázar and Clarice Lispector use the theme of rebellion and the antihero figure to give form to their views of contemporary life. Centering on several of the characters created by Cortázar and Lispector, Pereira argues that they both attempt to transcend social reality and gain access to the core of things, to discover essentials rather than deal in superficialities.

Pontiero, Giovanni. "The Drama of Existence in *Laços de família.*" *Studies in Short Fiction* 8, no. 1 (Winter 1977):256–67. Notes the widespread critical belief that Lispector does her best work in the story form. Outlines the parallels between Camus's sense of Absurdity and the ways it appears in Lispector's work. Offers brief summaries of the stories in this collection and concludes by commenting on such aspects of Lispector's work as style, characterization, plot, and thematics.

———. "Excerpts from the *Chronicles of the Foreign Legion.*" *Review 24,* 1980, pp. 37–43. Has a clear and perceptive introductory statement about both Lispector and *A legião estrangeira,* one of Lispector's most important yet oddly overlooked works. Also features accurate translations of several nonfiction pieces from this collection that show Lispector explaining herself as a writer. The selections are among the most revealing for anyone interested in how Lispector viewed her own work, especially her sense of style and structuring.

———. Introduction to *Family Ties.* Austin: University of Texas Press, 1972, pp. 13–23. A somewhat altered version of the article that appeared in *Studies in Short Fiction,* but with expanded discussions of the stories.

———. "Testament of Experience: Some Reflections on Clarice Lispector's Last Narrative *A hora da estrela.*" *Ibero-Amerikanisches Archiv,* n. s. 10, no. 1 (1984):13–22. In an excellent article, Pontiero discusses how Lispector focuses in this highly regarded novel not so much on the obvious sociological implications of poverty but on the hidden psychological ones. Notes how Lispector narrates "from within," how she blurs the distinction between herself and Macabéa (the main character in the novel), and how her portrait of Macabéa has the "primitive innocence" of Jorge Amado's heroines and the "disconcerting frankness" of Dalton Trevisan's. Says the novel has a moral of universal significance.

Rabassa, Gregory. His translation of and introduction to *The Apple in the Dark.* New York: Alfred A. Knopf, 1967, ix–xvi. An excellent summation of Lispector's life up to 1961 and her importance as a writer working within the modernist tradition in Brazil. Places her in the wider context of Latin American literature as well. Offers a substantial and perceptive analysis of *A maçã no escuro* and evaluates it in terms of Lispector's career up to its publication.

———. *Encyclopedia of World Literature in the Twentieth Century.* New York: Frederick Ungar, 1975, 4:220–23. A brief summary of Lispector's life and place in Brazilian literature. Shows Lispector's similarities with Guimarães Rosa as well as with Julio Cortázar and Gabriel García Márquez. Sees style as separating her work from theirs, however, and notes how her style is well suited to the interior monologue, which she uses so much. Says Lispector stands with Rosa and Nélida Piñon as one who did much to revise Brazilian fiction after World War II.

Reis, Fernando G. "Quem tem mêdo de Clarice Lispector." *Revista Civilização Brasileira*, no. 17 (January and February 1968):225–34. Citing the difficult philosophic foundations of Lispector's work, Reis notes how her fiction has intimidated many people. Performing an analytic overview of several of her novels and stories, Reis sees her style as an organic extension of her subject matter. He says that the two structural lines of her work are the microscopic/individual and the cosmic/universal, and that her themes reflect a concern with the eternal conflicts of the human condition.

Reis, Roberto. "Além do humano." *Minas Gerais Suplemento Literário*, December 5, 1981, pp. 6–7. Reis focuses on one of Lispector's most controversial works, *A paixão segundo G. H.*, and shows how its existential ethos stems from its author's handling of language, her sense of how the epiphany allows her to depict her characters' psychological ebb and flow, and how they experience their own private passions. He also shows the importance of animals (in this case a cockroach) to her work.

Rocha, Diva Vasconcelos. "*Laços de família* ou a enunciação do humor." *Minas Gerais Suplemento Literário*, May 25, 1974, p. 3. An interesting examination of the role humor, perhaps the least-studied aspect of Lispector's work, plays in the story "Laços de família." Rocha argues that humor, absurdist and, ultimately, tragic in nature (and deriving chiefly from the failure of language to communicate effectively), actually structures the text of the story.

———. "Paixão e morte do narrador segundo o narrador." *Minas Gerais Suplemento Literário*, November 22, 1980, p. 2; November 29, 1980, p. 4. Discusses the various voices (Macabéa's, Lispector's, those of the other characters) and the various levels of interpretation that compose the text of *A hora da estrela*. Also addresses the question of the novel's possibly autobiographical structuring, including Lispector's own background and her thoughts on how and why she writes.

Rossi, Maria Helena. "Os sucessivos e rodondos vácuos." *Minas Gerais Suplemento Literário*, nos. 779 and 780 (September 12, 1981):14–15. Basing her comments on Lispector's "social novel," *A hora da estrela*, Rossi shows how Lispector draws the reader into an active participation in the creation of the text that is the novel itself. Shows how Lispector attempted to integrate her social conscience, here concerning Brazil's troubled Northeast, with her penchant for technical ingenuity.

Sá, Olga de. "Clarice Lispector: Processos criativos." *Revista Iberoamericana* 50, no. 126 (January–March 1984):259–80. Focusing primarily on *Perto do coração selvagem*, Sá brings several current narratological critics to bear on Lispector's poetically based texts. Citing narrative theories advanced by such critics as Meyerhoff, Pouillon, Barthes, and Haroldo de Campos, Sá points out the "metalinguistic perspective" of the typical Lispectorian narrator. Interesting application of important narrative theorists to Lispector's fiction.

Seniff, Dennis. "Self-Doubt in Clarice's *Laços de família.*" *Luso-Brazilian Review* 14, no. 2 (Winter 1977):199–208. Notes the philosophical orientation of the stories in *Laços de família* but argues that Lispector's artistic (rather than philosophic) skill lies in her ability to "crystalize" her characters' moments of "self-examination." Argues, too, that each story follows a pattern of psychological equilibrium, external disruption, and an attempt at reaching a new equilibrium. Includes some interesting observations about "femininity" (and how it is portrayed) in Lispector's fiction.

Severino, Alexandrino E. "Major Trends in the Development of the Brazilian Short Story." *Studies in Short Fiction* 8, no. 1 (Winter 1971):199–208. A concise survey of the Brazilian short story from Machado de Assis up to the present day. Cites Lispector (along with Osman Lins and Guimarães Rosa) as figuring prominently among a group of writers who have changed, thematically and technically, the nature and form of the contemporary Brazilian short story.

Szklo, Gilda Salem. "O conto 'O búfalo' de *Laços de família* e a questão da escrita em Clarice Lispector." *Minas Gerais Suplemento Literário,* March 31, 1979, p. 5. Features an analysis, psycholinguistic in nature, of "The Buffalo" by comparing it to *A paixão segundo G. H.* Focuses on the parallels between the buffalo and the cockroach. Szklo also notes the crucial aspect of language in Lispector's story, in particular her tendency to construct and deconstruct personalities via language. Shows how Lispector's basic technique in "The Buffalo" (and in *A paixão segundo G. H.*) is to depict the painful process of psychic rebirth through self-confrontation and self-realization.

Index